CHURCH
PURCHASING
PROCEDURES

CHURCH BUSINESS MANAGEMENT SERIES

CHURCH PURCHASING PROCEDURES

Julian Feldman

and Contributing Author

G. Henry Richert

PRENTICE-HALL, INC.
Englewood Cliffs, New Jersey

This book is affectionately
and gratefully dedicated to Nan.

Library of Congress Catalog Card Number: 64-7827

Printed in the United States of America. T 13370

PRENTICE-HALL INTERNATIONAL, INC., *London*
PRENTICE-HALL OF AUSTRALIA, PTY., LTD., *Sydney*
PRENTICE-HALL OF CANADA, LTD., *Toronto*
PRENTICE-HALL OF INDIA (PRIVATE) LTD., *New Delhi*
PRENTICE-HALL OF JAPAN, INC., *Tokyo*

ACKNOWLEDGMENTS

IF THIS BOOK is helpful in achieving sound management of our churches and synagogues, it will be to a considerable degree because of the valuable counsel, ideas, and labor of scores of friends and colleagues of many denominations and from many communities across the United States. They are responsible for much that is good in this volume, but I fear that I cannot shift to them any of the onus for omissions or errors that may have crept in.

Two friends and co-workers deserve a special word of gratitude: Professor G. Henry Richert, a dedicated Methodist layman and authority on the American marketing system, collaborated in writing sections of three chapters and made available at every stage of the production of this manuscript his considerable experience, sound judgment, and keen sense of the appropriate word and phrase. My colleague, Hugh G. E. Paull, Director of Business Administration of the First Baptist Church of Washington, D.C., contributed much to the original plan of this volume. He has also been most helpful in preparing the appended study guide.

A. L. McMillan, former Director of Purchasing for the City of New York, and Myron E. Schoen, director of the

5

Commission on Synagogue Administration of the Union of American Hebrew Congregations, New York, were most generous with their authoritative and friendly comments on parts of the manuscript.

The manuscript profited greatly also from the constructive suggestions of the following colleagues in the field of church and synagogue administration: Frank J. Adler, Temple B'nai Jehudah, Kansas City, Missouri; Don Baker, First Congregational Church of Los Angeles, California; William J. Baerdas, Jr., First Presbyterian Church, Philadelphia, Pennsylvania; Zeb E. Barnhardt, Centenary Methodist Church, Winston-Salem, North Carolina; Roy E. Berry, Trinity Methodist Church, Tallahassee, Florida; Nancy S. Collier, Queen Street Methodist Church, Kinston, North Carolina; Robert R. Doty, Broadway Baptist Church, Forth Worth, Texas.

Others who have been helpful are Dr. Max Feder, Temple Rodeph Sholom, New York City; John G. Fischer, Wayzata Community Church, Wayzata, Minnesota; Henry Fruhauf, Congregation Emanu-El of the city of New York; J. O. Hardin, West Market Street Methodist Church, Greensboro, North Carolina; E. C. Hubert, Trinity Episcopal Church, Tulsa, Oklahoma; Margaret P. Jones, West End Methodist Church, Nashville, Tennessee; Irving I. Katz, Temple Beth El, Detroit, Michigan; Leif R. Larson, Central Lutheran Church, Minneapolis, Minnesota; Beulah S. Monroe, Washington Street Methodist Church, Alexandria, Virginia; Walter Schauman, Third Baptist Church, Saint Louis, Missouri; W. L. Schwantes, Myers Park Baptist Church, Charlotte, North Carolina; E. N. Sherer, First Methodist Church, Tuscaloosa, Alabama; K. F. Smith, East Dallas Christian Church, Dallas, Texas; John Stangl, First Presbyterian Church, San Diego, California; Dean Willis, First Baptist Church, Dallas, Texas.

Dr. Norman Gerstenfeld, my own spiritual leader, was tremendously helpful to me in evaluating the total manuscript from the clergyman's point of view and specifically in reviewing the material on ethics. E. William Seaman, my associate Rabbi, also gave me meaningful evaluations of my material.

During more than a decade of service as a temple administrator, my congregation and I have profited greatly from the management expertise of many laymen. Such skill and knowledge as I have in the field of purchasing has been especially enhanced by my association with Michael J. Deutch, Jac J. Lehrman, David Wise, Jr., and Frank Wolfsheimer.

I am indebted also to the suggestions of Bernard Chasman, a lay committee worker in Dayton, Ohio. Also to Arnold Levy and William C. Koplovitz, dedicated lay leaders of the Washington Hebrew Congregation.

The capable and patient members of the office staff of the Washington Hebrew Congregation over an 18-month period, spent innumerable hours on various drafts of the manuscript and the voluminous correspondence. I am particularly grateful to Mesdames Edna Maurer, Miriam Baller, Bert Becker, Bernice Nasoff, Evelyn Passwell, and Violet Heitzman.

Finally, each member of my family not only gave patient understanding throughout the writing process but supplied much needed help in all phases of the work. My wife took time from her own professional obligations to gather and organize the material, prepare the bibliography, and take care of a thousand and one details in connection with the manuscript preparation and editing. My eldest son, Reid, was extremely helpful in physical preparation and editing. My daughter, Lauren, and my son, Daniel, also participated in various of the production chores.

EDITOR'S INTRODUCTION

THE SERIES of books in which this volume is included was prepared for all who seek new insight and specific guidance in administering business affairs of churches. These books represent the most comprehensive publishing project ever completed in the field of church business management.

Each book in the series is based on two major premises: First, if churches are to accomplish their purposes effectively, their business affairs must be managed as well as, or better than, those of other organizations. Second, since churches are service-rendering rather than profit-making, and because of their voluntary nature and the trustee relationship involved, their business policies and practices must differ in certain respects from those of commercial enterprises—and these differences must be clearly identified and thoroughly understood.

These books are intended (1) to help clergy and laity develop additional competence for effective stewardship of church business responsibilities, (2) to provide stimulation and practical suggestions for professional career employment as business managers of churches and related non-profit organizations, and (3) to make available an educational

8

basis for strengthening the role of pastors as chief administrators of individual churches.

In planning, organizing, and evaluating this series of books the editor was confronted with certain basic questions to which explicit answers had not been published. What *is* church business management? What is it *for?* What is it *not?* What is it *not* for? What are its boundaries? The following tentative definition by the editor is the result of his pioneer effort to delineate and identify this field:

> *Church Business Management* is the science and art of administering church program development, financial resources, physical facilities, office services, staff personnel, and public relations, in accordance with the most effective standards of religious stewardship. Included in this concept are such managerial processes as forecasting, planning, organizing, delegating, controlling, evaluating, and reporting. Management of a church's business responsibilities is a facilitating function to be regarded not as an end in itself but as an important means to a worthy end.

Illustrations of what may be considered "church business management" have come from congregations that have added a professional business manager to the employed staff. A carefully written job description for such a staff member usually can help any church identify the business functions that are essential in establishing and attaining its distinctive purposes. Such job descriptions should, and often do, represent the business manager as a professional consultant and resource leader in helping church officers and staff, both volunteers and employees, perform their administrative duties in relation to the ministry of:

1. *Program Development*—planning, organizing, and scheduling all appropriate means available to the church for achieving its objectives and goals

2. *Financial Management*—budgeting, obtaining, safeguarding, disbursing, and accounting for all financial resources
3. *Property Management*—using, maintaining, and acquiring physical facilities such as buildings and grounds, furniture, and equipment
4. *Office Management*—providing systematic programs of scheduling, communicating, and recording services to facilitate achievement of administrative functions
5. *Personnel Management*—determining and describing staff positions; enlisting, assigning, and training nonprofessional staff, both volunteers and employees; developing and maintaining staff morale
6. *Public Relations*—communicating the church's concept of its purposes, its programs, its accomplishments, its potentialities, and its needs

Church business management as viewed in this light, and when applied creatively through proper use of collaborative and democratic procedures, is a significant phase of a meaningful spiritual ministry. How successfully and effectively the author of each book in this series has amplified the foregoing philosophy and specifications each reader will, of course, judge for himself.

For invaluable advice and practical assistance throughout the planning and execution stages of this endeavor the editor is especially grateful to Dr. Nathan A. Baily, Dean of American University's School of Business Administration. Dean Baily's keen interest and able leadership stimulated the establishment of The American University Center for Church Business Management while facilitating the development of this series of books.

Clyde W. Humphrey
General Editor

Washington, D.C.

CONTENTS

Chapter 1

INTRODUCTION TO CHURCH PURCHASING

WHY A BOOK ON CHURCH PURCHASING

FIFTY YEARS AGO, many of our grandparents would have considered the idea of a book devoted entirely to procedures of church purchasing as somewhat irreligious. Even one generation ago, such an idea would have been greeted with only slightly less shock. Quite likely, it would have been accompanied by a wry smile and a critical comment on the increasing secularization of churches and the encroachment of materialistic values into the spiritual domain.

Today, however, few thinking people would criticize churches and synagogues[1] for seeking to follow, where appropriate, the best practices in purchasing goods and services. Many church lay leaders used to apply a double standard: they would seek out fervently the latest procedures of scientific management for their business enterprises, but would shy away from any attempt to apply them to the business functions of their church. Now, most laymen and clergymen alike have come to recognize that a church does not necessarily desecrate its spiritual mission by operating in an efficient and rational manner. On the

[1] Throughout this book the term "church" is used generically to include congregations of all religious faiths, Jewish as well as Christian.

13

contrary, there is a growing recognition of the fact that judicious use of many widely accepted procedures of business management is essential if churches are to make their most effective impact upon our daily lives. Churches have the right to be the beneficiaries of all the material resources that committed laymen can give them. This means not only their tithes and offerings but also their gifts of methods of managing these contributions.

Churches are part of the essential structure of our society. If they are to bring their spirit to bear upon the manners and mores of people in their daily lives, they must speak the idiom of the people and organize themselves into a recognizable structural reflection of the society in which they exist. Churches and other agencies of our society have a reciprocal relationship. The church, at its best, infuses society with the divine spirit and moral wisdom of the ages. The primacy of this function, in turn, entitles the church to be the beneficiary of the secular and material blessings that it needs to perform its mission most effectively.

It is important to remember, however, that the purposes, objectives, and goals of a church are different from those of a commercial enterprise. A business procedure that is good for a profit-making organization may not be entirely appropriate to the needs of the church. To the extent that it can be adapted to the special goals and program of the church, it can and should be used, but we should not hesitate to change or discard ideas, methods, and procedures that are out of place in the church.

In this book, we attempt to present a workable purchasing program that will be useful to most churches. To the extent that they are applicable, we have drawn heavily on tested principles and procedures adopted and applied by business and industry. However, many managerial controls and procedures that are used successfully in large business firms are not suitable for churches. By the same token, many of the special techniques and procedures that we recommend as being especially appropriate in the context of church purchasing may seem strange indeed to the purchasing agent of a commercial firm.

Systematic purchasing for a church is not an end in itself. Materials, services, and supplies are bought because they are needed. Their primary purpose in a church is to implement and to facilitate the work of the church. Savings realized through effective purchasing can be used in acquiring a larger volume of needed items or in making available a greater number of dollars for the primary program goals of the church.

DEVELOPMENT OF CHURCH PURCHASING

In the early days of our Republic, most items that a church consumed were fabricated or improvised on the spot or donated by members of the congregation. Management of these goods, even in the largest churches, was assigned to an untrained sexton or to a harried clergyman whose principal records, as likely as not, were notations stuck into his hat.

But in today's complex society, the church has multiplied its needs for goods and services. These must be bought in the open market at constantly inflated prices; this has dramatized and focused attention on the need for use of intelligent purchasing procedures in the church.

Purchasing used to be a relatively simple matter in all aspects of our life. After all, people have been buying goods and services for a long time; but the way we perform the purchasing process has changed considerably. Modern purchasing in every area, including the church, calls for the application of a degree of human understanding, technical judgment, and administrative ability that could not have been imagined a century ago.

WHAT DOES A CHURCH PURCHASE

There are three basic categories of purchase for churches:

1. *MRO Items.* These are the standard "maintenance, repair, and operation" items. Maintenance items include such things as janitor supplies, cleaning wax, soap, and electric light bulbs. Repair items are self-explanatory: a new starter for a fluorescent fixture, a high-wattage bulb for a motion-picture projector, tape for rebinding prayer books, new blades for lawn mowers. Operating items include crayons and construction paper for the Sunday School's primary grades, candles for the altar, robes for the minister—the infinite variety of material items that together make it possible for ministers and laymen to serve their congregations and the larger community.

2. *Services.* A few generations ago, the church that went outside its own membership or minister's office to purchase services was rare indeed. In today's specialized society, however, few churches can exist without the paid services of numerous contractors. Trucking, painting, and building alterations are some of the more common services required. Maintenance contracts for air conditioning and heating equipment, and service contracts for office equipment such as typewriters and duplicating machines, are now routine.

Increasingly, also, churches are finding out that the use of specialists can often save them much extra effort and money. Many churches contract out their window washing, pest control, landscaping, and other housekeeping functions. In its broadest sense, the category of services can include even new construction.

3. *Equipment.* In buying equipment, our primary concern is with the durability, suitability, and the general over-all quality of the article. These factors, in most cases, are far more important than price, although we should guard against a tendency to get a higher quality than is necessary to do the job adequately. Few items acquired through the church purchasing process are more important than equipment. Equipment generally represents a long-term investment of large amounts of capital. Moreover, the amounts and kinds of equipment in the church will determine to a considerable extent the church's operational procedures and efficiency. This includes building maintenance equipment, such as floor scrubbers and polishers; office and mail room equipment, such as typewriters, addressing machines, duplicators, folding machines and postage meters; also such specialized items as coin counters, and motion picture and slide projectors for the school.

WHO IS INVOLVED IN CHURCH PURCHASING

Many people are concerned with church purchasing. Ministers, business managers, board chairmen, board members, deacons, treasurers, financial secretaries, finance chairman, trustees, office secretaries, budget officers—and others are involved in spending church money and in acquiring the materials needed by churches. Every person involved in purchasing for the church should base his actions on knowledge and purpose rather than thoughtlessness and casualness in order that the monies spent provide the strongest possible support of the church's mission and programs.

This would be essential in any organization. In a church, which has such a vital responsibility to both God and man, anything less can be considered sacrilegious.

Chapter 2

ORGANIZING THE CHURCH PURCHASING PROGRAM

PURPOSES OF CHURCH PURCHASING

THE EFFECTIVENESS of any church can be greatly influenced by the way it obtains its material requirements. It is therefore important that the church know exactly what objectives it seeks to achieve through its system of purchasing procedures.

When we buy for ourselves, our motivations and our objectives are quite simple and easily definable: we are satisfying a personal need, desire, or whim. Often our motives are neither logical nor economical; but they are satisfactory to us because they meet criteria we have established for that particular purchase. In personal buying, we can often afford the luxury of an irrational choice because psychological satisfactions are frequently just as important as value, durability, and other objective criteria.

However, when we purchase for the church, we have no right or justification for using the casual approach and the subjective values of the personal-choice method. A major objective of purchasing is to get an adequate *quid pro quo* for each expended dollar. Churches are not, and should not be, businesses, but in acquiring the things they must have to accomplish their objectives, they sometimes function like a business. Purchasing deserves to be handled in the most effective way possible in order to protect the best interests of the church.

Church purchasing may be described most simply as a system for supplying the church with the items it needs. More specifically, in church purchasing we seek to buy for the church "the right thing, in the right quality, in the right quantity, at the right time, at the right price, from the right vendor . . ." [1]

This suggests a problem. What is right and what is proper? It is easy enough to say that we must purchase the "right thing" or the "proper thing," but who determines what is "right" or "proper," and how does he do it? Sometimes the determination is made for the buyer by situations beyond his control, but in most cases the answers to what is right and proper must be found by the individual who is doing the purchasing. His judgment depends in such cases on his understanding of the needs of the users, on the conditions of the market, on his experience, on his intuitive balancing of needs and capabilities, and, in the final analysis, on common sense.

RESPONSIBILITIES AND DUTIES OF THE PURCHASING AGENT

The responsibility of the church purchasing agent is, of course, to procure the goods and services that will satisfy the justified desires and needs of the users of these goods and services—the committee or commission chairman, the director of education, the minister of music, the chairman of the board of deacons, the pastor, and others.

The person in charge of purchasing for a church must:

[1] A. L. McMillan, *The Art of Purchasing* (New York: Exposition Press, 1959), p. 17.

1. Anticipate the needs of users of materials within the church family.
2. Standardize and simplify products used by various programs of the church.
3. Maintain continuity of supply.
4. Maintain a minimum investment in inventory, consistent with safety and continuity of operations as well as with budgetary objectives. Any overinvestment in inventory is translated ultimately into curtailment of program objectives of the church.
5. Avoid duplication, waste, and obsolescence.
6. Maintain standards of quality of materials, based on suitability of use.
7. Procure items at the lowest cost, consistent with safety and economic advantage.
8. Ascertain what equipment and supplies have been declared surplus by any church department; move such surplus supplies and equipment from one department to another where maximum use can be made of them, or dispose of this material to the maximum advantage of the church.

ELEMENTS OF
THE PROCUREMENT PROCEDURE

When we purchase for private use, we perform essentially four basic actions: we decide what we want; we decide where we want to get it; we buy it; and we use it.

When we translate these actions into purchasing for churches, we have to refine them and define them far more precisely. There are 17 procedural steps in every purchase transaction. A good system for church purchasing must provide for each of these elements and insure that each of them is accomplished effectively and systematically. These elements are:

1. Ascertainment of need: the decision by someone that something is needed.
2. Statement of the character or quality of the item needed.
3. Statement of the amount of the article or service desired.
4. Determination of when the item is needed.
5. Transmission of the purchase request from the person or department needing it to the person who is responsible for acquiring it.
6. Consolidation, where possible, of requests from various using departments.
7. Seeking out possible vendors, evaluating them, and negotiating with them for acquisition of the goods.
8. Determination of routing and delivery instructions.
9. Analysis of proposals, final selection of the vendor, and placement of the order.
10. Following up on the order to insure shipment in adequate time for most effective use.
11. Receiving the item and checking the invoice.
12. Inspecting the goods.
13. Completion of the record and certification for payment.
14. Payment for the goods.
15. Storage of the goods received.
16. Inventory of the items procured.
17. Research into the way the items are used to determine the effectiveness of the purchasing activity.

Each of the foregoing 17 steps is an essential part of the purchasing procedure. Each is performed, either consciously or unconsciously, when buying for the church. To the extent that these steps are carried out effectively, the church is well served.

THE CASE FOR CENTRALIZED PURCHASING

In a church having a centralized purchasing system, no commitment for any purchase is final until approved by the official who is responsible for coordinating the purchasing activities.

By contrast, a decentralized plan gives to numerous officials—the pastor, the director of education, the music director, individual Sunday School teachers, office personnel, custodians, and other users of material—the authority to make purchases of items necessary in carrying out their assigned jobs.

What are some of the advantages of a system in which no purchasing commitment is final until approved by a single responsible purchasing official?

1. *Centralized purchasing promotes buying economy and efficiency:*

   a. The purchasing agent can pool the requirements of various departments, taking advantage of quantity discounts and lower unit costs.

   b. Central purchasing can obtain shipping cost reductions by combining shipments.

   c. Better planning of the total purchase requirements of the church is made possible.

   d. Better budgetary and accounting controls of departmental expenditures are provided.

   e. There are more consistent possibilities of taking cash discounts by prompt handling of vendors' invoices through a central office.

   f. Administrative costs are reduced through the elimination of multiple purchasing records, procedure, and personnel time.

   g. Better delivery service usually can be obtained through a central receiving facility.

   h. Better service by suppliers may be obtained when they deal with only one individual.

   i. Inventories are reduced through closer supervision of stocks, better judgments regarding the quantities of materials in each purchase order, and better use of the available supply through transfers and substitutions within and among departments.

j. Centralized supervision is provided for inspection of deliveries, systematic storage, and distribution of stock.

k. Vendor relations are improved because suppliers will have been carefully selected by the central purchasing agent, and follow-up of such purchase is more easily obtained through a central, responsible officer.

l. Centralized purchasing permits the adoption of standard specifications for certain items that are in common use by more than one department, resulting in more uniform quality and less variety of material, supplies, and equipment.

2. *Centralized purchasing promotes better use of staff personnel:*

Perhaps the most telling advantages of a centralized purchasing system comes in the way it permits the church to make better use of its staff personnel:

a. By concentrating the purchasing function in a single responsible officer, the other people of the church are freed from much of the time-consuming research and the administrative details involved in purchasing.

b. By concentrating on purchasing, the purchasing agent develops a body of special knowledge, skills, and procedures, which in turn results in better procurement. The purchasing agent becomes proficient in locating suppliers of specialized items as well as the more common ones.

c. A centralized purchasing system facilitates participation in a cooperative purchasing program on an interchurch basis.

d. Inspections can be performed more thoroughly in the using departments because they are relieved of direct buying responsibility and of psychological involvement with suppliers.

e. Better administrative controls are assured throughout the church, since one person or department is directly responsible to the governing board for implementing the policy aspects of the purchasing procedure. Also, there is only one complete set of records pertaining to all purchasing transactions, commitments, and expenditures.

The foregoing advantages are neither universal nor automatic. Impressive as they are, the advantages of a centralized purchasing program can be sabotaged by improper application of central authority.

For example, by not considering all factors when combining the needs of different departments, we may increase the cost rather than decrease it. Some years ago, the author discovered what he thought was a wasteful practice of purchasing small, dime-store rolls of transparent tape for the teachers of the Religious School. Since the larger rolls, which cost much less per yard, obviously were being used with greater economy in the business office, there seemed to be no question but that similar savings could be effected if the Religious School teachers used the same size tape. The school superintendent was dubious about making this change, pointing out that the small dime-store size was much more convenient for the teachers to use. However, in the interest of institutional economy and harmony, she acceded. Six months later, the author discovered to his chagrin that the disbursements for transparent tape had more than doubled. The teachers had been inclined to husband the short roll and used the tape only where essential. With the large rolls of tape came the implied acquiescence of the administrator in a more generous consumption of transparent tape for countless new uses with the longest possible strips. A return to the shorter rolls brought a prompt return of frugality.

This is only one example of how the intrusion of the human element can sometimes limit the effectiveness of the centralized purchasing program. Some other potential cautions should be observed in administering a purchasing program. There is a danger that the central purchasing agent will create excessive paperwork and force the using departments to pay too much attention to minute and unimportant details. Red tape is always resented and it sets up a psychological barrier to cooperation between the purchasing agent and the using departments. Moreover, more paperwork can result in delay.

The central purchasing agent sometimes can place too much emphasis on monetary savings as compared to aesthetic and other intangible values, which also can be important in the church.

Here are certain cautions to bear in mind in a centralized church purchasing operation:

1. Centralized purchasing can experience difficulty in achieving proper timing and communication between the using departments and thereby result in loss of efficiency.
2. In case of emergency, a centralized purchasing set-up could result in delay in acquiring some urgently needed goods or services.
3. By relieving such specialists as the education and music directors of certain phases of the purchasing function in their specialized fields, the church could be deprived of some of the technical know-how available to it.
4. Centralized bulk purchasing may create the need for central storage facilities that might be unavailable.
5. Centralized purchasing for a large church can create problems in ordering, receiving, inventory, and distribution.
6. Centralized purchasing systems frequently require the

outlay of considerable sums of money to "stock up" the central supply.

7. Finally, centralized purchasing, if conducted in a cold, impersonal manner, could harm internal public relations in a church by offending some members who are potential suppliers.

Each of these objections has the germ of validity and should serve as a warning flag in the administration of centralized purchasing. However, each can be overcome by tactful effort on the part of the purchasing agent who demonstrates his efficiency, resourcefulness, and cooperativeness, *provided* he is backed up by the governing board and by his colleagues on the church staff.

CHOOSING A PURCHASING AGENT FOR THE CHURCH

The size of the church and its budget, and the number of professionals on the staff, will determine the type of organization and the place in which the purchasing function can be centralized. Where a church is fortunate enough to have the services of a professional business manager, the functions of centralized purchasing are naturally and normally assigned here. In the office of the business manager, we can bring together at one central point the total responsibility for coordinating the purchasing of all materials and services by all church officials, departments, and affiliates.

Where there is no professional administrator, the task of serving as purchasing agent inevitably devolves upon either the pastor or one of the other ministers, or a lay person in the church. Unhappily for all concerned, the choice in too many cases is the pastor. In virtually every case, this is a mistake. Such an assignment must distract a clergyman from his spiritual duties, and to this extent the congregation is deprived of his ministry.

A layman usually should be selected to perform the purchasing function in preference to a minister. He might be the chairman or a member of the building and grounds committee. He might be one of the officers, such as the financial secretary or the treasurer. But the author's opinion is that it is usually wisest to place the purchasing responsibility into the hands of a competent and responsible layman who can arrange to devote adequate time to this important endeavor. For purposes of this book, we call this person the "church purchasing agent."

The ideal church purchasing agent will, first of all, have an unquestioned dedication to the congregation. Moreover, a pleasant personality is as essential in purchasing as in any field of human endeavor. The purchasing agent's work habits should be characterized by thoroughness and an ability to pay attention to details. He must be firm but not inflexible, a cooperative team worker, and instinctively ethical. From a practical point of view, the person to whom this task is assigned should have adequate time to carry out his duties properly and should have a background of appropriate training and experience.

A church purchasing agent should be qualified by experience and formal education in business management, including a thorough grounding in basic principles and procedures of procuring, storing, distributing, and accounting. He should have some knowledge of market conditions, current prices, qualities of materials, traffic procedures, business law, specifications, and sources of supply. He should be able to learn about the reputation of suppliers and their ability to serve the needs of his church, and he should be aware of the sharp practices sometimes used by vendors.

The church purchasing agent should have the ability to maintain a cooperative relationship with vendors without succumbing to their blandishments. He should deal with the public in a courteous and pleasing manner and be able to handle complaints tactfully and without causing unnecessary criticism. He should know how to get people to work together effectively, how to keep records, how to make investigations and prepare reports, and how to assist in the preparation of specifications. He must be honest, resourceful, and intelligent. He must have keen business judgment, skill, and discrimination.

If this sounds like the definition of the ideal church business manager, we have made our point. Effective performance of the purchasing function is one of the most important phases of church business management. The qualifications that make for success in church purchasing will virtually assure successful performance of the other business functions of a church. Although many churches are not yet able to employ a professional administrator, these same qualifications should be sought when selecting the layman to do the purchasing.

FUNCTIONS OF A CHURCH PURCHASING AGENT

There are four principal areas in which the church purchasing agent serves his congregation:

1. BASIC INFORMATION SOURCES: It is the responsibility of the purchasing agent to keep all necessary records with regard to purchases, prices, stocks, rates of consumption, specifications, catalogs, and source data.
2. RESEARCH: It is generally the responsibility of the church purchasing agent to find out as much as he can about the market of the goods and services needed by the church, to discover information about the materials that are used, make cost analyses, research supply sources,

where necessary examine supplier's facilities, develop new supply sources to replace those that become inadequate, and, finally, develop alternate materials and uses as required.

3. PROCUREMENT: Here is the crux of the church purchasing agent's job. He is responsible for:

   a. Receiving requests from other areas within the church.
   b. Securing quotations on prices.
   c. Analyzing such quotations.
   d. Choosing among open market purchase opportunities.
   e. Scheduling purchases and delivery.
   f. Interviewing salesmen.
   g. Negotiating contracts.
   h. Issuing purchase orders.
   i. Checking the legal provisions of the contracts or seeing to it that these checks are made by qualified persons.
   j. Following-up on orders to insure adequate delivery on time.
   k. Checking that materials are received and are in good order.
   l. Verifying invoices.
   m. Maintaining correspondence with vendors.

4. MATERIALS MANAGEMENT: Even after the materials are received, the church purchasing agent still has responsibilities for:

   a. Maintaining the minimum stocks of necessary goods.
   b. Maintaining inventory records.
   c. Analyzing inventory practices to insure that available cash is not tied up unduly and stocks are not too low for continuous operation.
   d. Consolidating requirements among the using departments.
   e. Avoiding excess stocks and obsolescence.
   f. Accounting for returnable containers.
   g. Disposing of surplus materials.

LEGAL RELATIONSHIPS
OF A CHURCH PURCHASING AGENT

Whenever a church asks a person to represent and act for it, this person becomes its agent. In the case of a purchasing agent for a church, the agency relationship is created by his employment or appointment to perform the purchasing function.

It is important to distinguish between *general and special agents*. A *general agent* is one who is authorized to act for the church in all church matters. By implication, greater powers are conferred upon a general agent than upon one who is authorized to represent the church in only a limited way. In a church, the ministers, the business manager, or anyone officially designated as the purchasing agent ordinarily would be considered general agents. On the other hand, chairmen of commissions and committees, directors of departments, and laymen having more limited responsibilities, would be considered *special agents*.

Authority of a Church Purchasing Agent: Authority may be either "express," "apparent," or "implied." *Express authority* is conferred by a formal contract, or a job description.

Apparent authority may be acquired when church officials act in a manner that leads vendors to believe that certain laymen are authorized agents of the church. For example, a Sunday School teacher may charge to the church account certain supplies for class use, or a church secretary may charge typewriter paper for the office. If the church approves and pays for these purchases, the church has accepted the agency status by ratification. It is therefore quite important that we define in writing for all church employees and officials their precise responsibilities and the precise limits of their authority to act for the church.

The third form of authority is *implied authority*. We assume that it is the general intent of the church to give all church officials ample opportunity to perform their functions by every proper means at their command. As a result, the purchasing agent's implied authority can be construed to be very broad, so long as it does not conflict with any authority expressly denied him. This does not mean, however, that any person can capriciously commit and obligate the church without any limitation. When an agent goes beyond his authority in making a contract, the principal is not bound. The agent is personally liable for any deception, fraud, or other tort committed by him while carrying on the principal's business. It is easy to see, therefore, why the degree of authority conferred upon different persons should be made clear to vendors and all others doing business with the church.

Authority of the Vendor's Agent: While we are reviewing the kinds of authority possessed by a church representative, we should also consider the authority of the persons with whom a purchasing agent deals in his procurement activities. Generally, the purchasing agent deals with the vendor's salesmen. Although the salesman represents his company, his authority as an agent is somewhat limited. *He is legally regarded as a representative who solicits business for his company, and not a legal agent authorized to conclude a contract of sale. This means that statements and offers the salesmen may make are not valid and binding until they are confirmed by the vendor's office.* Similarly, advertisements of vendors have been held by courts to be invitations for offers, rather than offers themselves.

Duties of an Agent: From a legal point of view, the

duties of the purchasing agent in a church are related to the following three basic obligations:

1. *Obedience to Instructions.* He is expected to perform his duties in a manner prescribed by the governing board of the church.
2. *Acting in Good Faith.* The relation between principal and agent is based on mutual trust and confidence. The purchasing agent "cannot serve two masters": that is, he cannot act for both the church and a third party unless this is clearly understood beforehand. Should the purchasing agent have an interest in some firm that is a possible supplier, this should be fully made known to church officials.
3. *Use of Necessary Skill and Competency.* Under the law, an agent is required to possess and to use the prudence, skill, and diligence required in the proper conduct of the business entrusted to him. If he fails to exercise the skill and good judgment expected of him, and the church sustains a loss, he may be personally liable for the loss. A person appointed to such a position is required to personally use these talents. He may not indiscriminately assign to another the independent exercise of discretion or judgment unless his principal has approved this step. Naturally, this does not prevent the agent from delegating clerical or mechanical duties to others, as long as he retains essential supervisory control.

EVALUATING THE PERFORMANCE OF A CHURCH PURCHASING AGENT

Evaluations of church purchasing performance are almost impossible to make. Nor are they necessarily desirable. An overemphasis on monetary savings can actually decrease the effectiveness of the purchasing department in insuring the acquisition of the best possible materials for serving the members of the congregation.

Probably the best measurement of the degree to which a church purchasing agent is fulfilling his responsibility is obtained by an adaptation of the principles and standards of purchasing practice advocated by the *National Association of Purchasing Agents* (NAPA), the professional organization of full-time specialists in this field. Paraphrasing in "church language" the announced principles of the NAPA, we can say that the basic principles of a good church purchasing program are:

1. To consider, first, the interests of his church in all transactions and to believe in and carry out the established policies of the church.
2. To be receptive to competent counsel from his pastor and other co-workers and to be guided by such counsel without impairing the dignity and responsibility of his office.
3. To buy without prejudice, seeking to obtain the maximum ultimate value for each dollar of expenditure.
4. To strive consistently for knowledge of the materials and processes of manufacture and to establish practical methods for conduct of his office.
5. To subscribe to and work for honesty and truth in buying and selling, and to denounce all forms and manifestations of commercial bribery.
6. To accord a prompt and courteous reception, as far as conditions will permit, to all who call on a legitimate business mission.
7. To respect his obligations and to require that obligations to him and to his church be respected, consistent with good business practice.
8. To counsel and assist fellow church administrators and purchasing agents in the performance of their duties, whenever occasion permits.
9. To cooperate with all organizations and individuals engaged in activities designed to enhance the development and standing of church purchasing.

Chapter 3

STARTING THE
PURCHASE PROCEDURE—
EXPRESSION OF NEED

IN OUR personal purchasing habits, we sometimes indulge ourselves by buying some item to satisfy a casual whim or caprice. This is one luxury that the purchasing agent for a church can never permit himself. Every purchase for the church starts with an established "need."

DETERMINATION OF NEED

Generally speaking, the department that will ultimately use the goods and materials will determine the need. The director of music finds a new selection for the choir and thereby determines the need for an adequate number of copies of the music. The building manager, on the basis of inspection or in conformity with the planned maintenance program, decides to strip and wax the social hall floor. He thereby determines the need for a certain quantity of cleaning solvent and an appropriate amount of floor wax. The clerk-typist notices that her letters begin to appear dull and gray, and she determines the need for a new typewriter ribbon. The director of education, in his program planning and evaluation, decides he needs two new combination slide and film strip projectors and a new 16-millimeter motion-picture projector.

The determination of what has to be purchased comes then from:

a. *Personal observation:* The identification of a need by the individual in charge of an operating program, who decides that some item has to be purchased so that he can carry through his responsibility properly.

b. *Inventory analysis:* The determination that the supply of some item in regular use, such as mimeograph paper, has become so short that replenishment of the supply is necessary or desirable.

c. *Suggestions by salesmen:* Vendor's representatives who call on the business manager or purchasing agent can frequently apprise him of products, materials, or services that would enable the church to save time, effort, or money, or to perform some function more effectively.

d. *Internal research:* Whenever a new operating problem arises, an evaluation of ways of solving the problem or meeting a new responsibility will probably suggest new products or services that can be helpful. Thus, a new building fund campaign that results in the need to record and process several hundred new building fund pledge payments over a period of several years will pose a new problem that may suggest a new need for an additional set of ledger books; possibly a new "one-write" posting system, or even a new bookkeeping machine, a supply of pre-addressed, wallet-flap, postage-paid envelopes to make it convenient for each member of the congregation to send in his pledge payments on a periodic basis.

e. *Trade and professional publications:* Magazines in the office management field, or in the field of property management, education, or music, are a rich source of suggestions for new products and services.

PURCHASE AUTHORIZATION

Once a need has been identified, there must be some determination of the availability of resources to meet the need.

For some items, of course, an oral expression of need is sufficient authorization; a box of paper clips is casually drawn from a central office inventory; washroom dispensers are routinely kept filled with paper towels. But the purchase of a new motion-picture projector will usually require a much more formal authorization.

The determination of need ordinarily is made by the department that will ultimately use the material. Usually, also, the using department determines whether its funds are adequate to cover the need, or whether an additional appropriation must be requested. This is especially true of equipment and specialized supplies. It is less true for routine operating items such as office supplies, which may be handled from a central storage facility. Here, the determination might be made by a clerk who maintains the inventory record.

In any case, someone must determine whether funds are available to acquire the needed item. It may be a department head—or it may be a lay committee chairman. In a large church with a specialized professional staff, the lay committee head generally makes the basic budget request, but the administration of the budget for the department usually is in the hands of a paid professional. This means that the staff man has relatively complete freedom to decide whether a specific item is covered by the budget. In some cases, this responsibility is divided, with the professional making the decision on all purchases below a certain cost, while all items costing more than a stated dollar value

—$100, $250, or $500—requires the joint authorization of both the layman and the paid professional.

ANTICIPATION OF NEED

The budget, properly prepared, becomes a basic tool for the anticipation of needs. If adequate diligence has been given to budget preparation, the using departments will have anticipated realistically its needs not only for the repetitive, routine items, but also for special equipment and supplies that will be required to implement the programs and activities during the coming year. These items will then appear as individual lines in the final budget, if the budget is a detailed one, or in the worksheets and other supporting documents for the individual department budget.

For special projects, a bill of materials should be prepared, so that all items that may be needed during the coming budget year are listed, together with their probable costs. This serves as a guide to budget requirements, as well as an anticipatory purchase list. Thus, a close liaison must be maintained between the purchasing office and the using departments.

COMMUNICATION OF NEED—THE REQUISITION

The degree of formality and details of procedure may vary from congregation to congregation. They will also vary in degrees within each church. The fact remains, however, that the needs we have determined must be communicated to the person who makes the purchases on behalf of the church. The standard form of expression of this need is called the purchase requisition.

A purchase requisition may be either formal or informal. An oral request by the minister of music to obtain three additional music stands for the choir loft is one way of communicating a need. In many situations, such an informal requisition may be sufficient. The larger the church, however, the more detailed the budget, and the greater the number of items bought, the more formal must be the communication system. And it is here that we are more likely to find the printed or duplicated requisition form in use.

Typical simple purchase requisitions that can very adequately serve the needs of both the large and small church are shown as figures 1, 2, and 3.

Though the purchase requisition form need not be complex, it is the standard form of expression of need, and, as such, it becomes a fundamental device in the procedure of satisfying identified needs. The principles of good form design apply just as much to a church purchase requisi-

TOPS form 3243		Purchase Requisition	No. 263
			Date 10/20/64

Purchasing Department
Please purchase the following named items:

INDICATE SOURCE OF SUPPLY IF KNOWN

Quantity	Number	Description
3	gross	white chalk
25	reams	mimeograph paper, 20 lb

classroom use

When wanted nov. 1

To be filled in by Purchasing Dept.
Date ordered 10/22/64   Order No. 1234
From acme office supply Co.

For education Dept.   Approved Walter Abel

Figure 1. This typical purchase requisition form is available from commercial stationery supply houses. It may be purchased either in pads of alternating colors or in multipart sets. (Courtesy Tops Business Forms, Chicago, Ill.)

UNIVERSAL COMMUNITY CHURCH

REQUISITION

July 15 , 1964

Please furnish the following:

Stamps & postcards:	Total Amt:	Other items:
4¢ *1250*	$ *100.00*	
5¢ *500*	*25.00*	
double postcards *250*	*20.00*	
single postcards		

Requested by: *Jane Singer*   Chg. Budget Acct. No. *809*   Approved by: *George Doakes*

Figure 2. A simple requisition form like this one can be prepared in any church office on its own duplicating machinery. It is suitable both for items like postage, which are drawn from stock, as well as for items which are to be purchased. (Courtesy Washington Hebrew Congregation, Washington, D.C.)

tion as to any other document, wherever used. For instance:

1. Provision should be made for logical grouping of all information to be conveyed.
2. Typewriter spacing should be considered wherever a typewriter may be used in filling out the form.
3. The routing of the form should be indicated.
4. A standard size paper should be used, particularly where the form is to be reproduced within the church facilities.
5. Signature spaces should be provided.

Two copies would appear to be adequate for most church purchases: one to be retained in the using department or in the files of the person originating the request;

REQUISITION

UNIVERSAL COMMUNITY CHURCH   No. *647*

Music and Choir Department

Budget Item -405

Date *8/13/64*

Amount Needed	DESCRIPTION
6	*Music Stands, adjustable. (Same as last order, 6/15 requisition #162)*
	needed by: 12/18/64

Ordered by *John Warbler*
Choir Director

Approved by *Walter Abel*
Business Manager

Figure 3. Specially designed requisition forms such as this one can be prepared by the purchasing agent and provided by a local printer.

the other, to go to the purchasing agent, to be attached to a copy of the purchase order as part of the complete purchase record. In some cases, it might be desirable to keep a third copy in a numerical sequence file. However, the usefulness of a third copy is marginal, and we would prefer to keep to a minimum the number of copies of this form and most others.

If a numerical sequence file is used, it will, of course, be necessary to have a number on the requisition. These forms can be pre-numbered when they are bought from a commercial printer or supply house, or they can be pre-numbered by hand or by an inexpensive numbering machine if they are duplicated in the church office.

The authorization for the purchase should be clearly stated. Where the item is specifically provided for in the budget, a simple reference to this is adequate. In all other cases, a reference should be made to the primary budget group heading under which the account is being authorized. Depending on the policy in the individual church, the requisition should be signed by the head of the using department, by the lay chairman of the committee involved, or by some other official who has been given special authority to approve purchases up to specified dollar limits for the department concerned.

In most churches, the department head has basic responsibility for the budget item relating to his department. Even if a relatively small budget item is involved, he should know of all requisitions for which a charge will ultimately be made to his department. The best way for him to be aware of these charges and to be sure that budget funds are available is to be certain that he has signed all requisitions for items charged to his budget. However, this still does not relieve the church purchasing agent from reviewing each requisition against the available budgetary allotments.

In specifying quantities on the requisition form, it is important to be as specific as possible. To avoid confusion, one should state whether one wishes solvent delivered in six 5-gallon cans or a single drum of 30 gallons. Similarly, simple digits should be avoided. The figure "6" could be interpreted on a hasty reading as "6 items," or "6 sets" of items, or "6 cases" of certain items, or "6 dozen." If you mean to order 8 individual items, say "8 each," or "8 pcs.," or specify any other appropriate ordering unit—dozens, sets, cases, cartons, barrels.

When stating the time that the item is needed, a specific date is far more helpful than such noninformative terms as "now," "rush," "immediately." These terms appear on requisitions and purchase orders so frequently that professional purchasing agents and experienced vendors are seldom moved by the requisition's expression of urgency.

The requisition is the *message* from the user of a needed item to the person who is responsible for buying the item.

The degree of the purchasing agent's authority to adjust the terms of the requisition to meet the needs of economy, uniformity, or any other over-all set of values will depend in each case on church policy.

The purchasing agent who questions for the sake of questioning, who delays for the sake of exhibiting his authority, who quibbles over unimportant points, fails to fulfill his function properly. In fact, he is impeding rather than expediting the smooth flow of the purchasing operation. Discretion and tact are his stock in trade. He can inquire without being snoopy. He can question without being critical. He can verify without quibbling. He can offer new information that should be considered prior to making a purchase without being destructive and self-serving.

KEEPING IT SIMPLE

People who are not accustomed to thinking in terms of business organization tend to equate the words "systems and procedures" with red tape and needless complexity. This fear is partly justified, because all too often designers of forms and systems think in terms of providing a procedure that will cover every conceivable eventuality, no matter how unlikely. As a result, the number of pieces of paper is multiplied, to make sure that every person and department in the organization receives copies. Complexity usually is not necessary. The more simplified and basic the system, the better it is for efficiency, economy, and morale.

Many books on purchasing state as an infallible rule that every purchase begins with a written requisition. However, in the church, a requisition need not be a written document in every case. An oral request to a purchasing agent for a new letter tray or waste basket is just as much a requisition, provided the purchasing agent has heard the request and acted on it as is a 12-part form with

22 separate items of information to be entered and spaces for signature approvals.

THE REPEATING REQUISITION

This is a handy device for saving time and paperwork in connection with supply items that are kept in a central storage facility. Instead of issuing a new requisition for each item needed from central storage, the user can come in person or make a telephone request for an item—i.e., "one dozen of No. 2 pencils," or "a ream of bond paper," or "a bottle of type cleaner." The item and amount drawn from stores is noted on the repeating requisition, which is used over and over again. It can also be used as an inventory record (see Chapter 9). The typical repeating requisition is printed on a card form of substantial quality, with a sufficient number of lines to note 10, 20, 30 or more withdrawals, as well as all pertinent data with regard to specifications, sources and minimum reorder points, such as are discussed in Chapter 9. The use of the repeating requisition as a perpetual inventory card is most practical for the church in which the purchasing agent is the business manager, and where purchases frequently are handled by the person in charge of inventory control.

CONSOLIDATION OF NEEDS

This is one of the areas in which centralized purchasing for a church can prove its worth most dramatically. A central purchasing department is the only level at which consolidation of needs is practicable.

The church purchasing agent is in a position to plan a coordinated procurement operation for all items used by more than one department. Using departments are encouraged by the purchasing agent to prepare and forward requisitions for all items purchased on a regular basis. This should be done sufficiently in advance of their needs to take into account not only the normal lead time required for buying certain items, but also to provide adequate time for grouping purchases from various departments for similar items.

The purchasing agent is also able to identify items used by one department that are similar, if not identical, to those used by another department, and to standardize requirements. Thus, when one department forwards a requisition for an article used in any measurable quantity by another department, the purchasing agent is in a position to spot this potential consolidation, and may request the second department to anticipate its need for the item by preparing its requisition immediately, rather than somewhat later, as might normally have been done. Usually, each of the department heads affected will welcome such a consolidation when they discover that it leads to more effective use of the budget and permits each of them to buy more commodities and equipment with his budget allotment than might otherwise have been possible.

STANDARDIZATION OF REQUIREMENTS

Gregory Andanter, the choir director at Universal Community Church, regularly orders one variety of transparent mending tape in ¾-inch width. Cathy Catalog, the librarian, uses a similar kind of tape of another brand in a ¾-inch width for book mending. A third type of transparent tape is kept in stock for Sally Pert, Mabel Quick, and Diana Friendly—the three secretary-typists in the church office. Specification requirements for each of the three kinds of tape ordered are slightly different. But there is enough similarity that the alert purchasing agent will investigate the possibility of standardizing the specification in order to consolidate the needs of the three types of user. Perhaps he will find that a mending tape ½-inch wide will satisfy the needs of both the choir director and the librarian. The clerical personnel may find that the low-gloss mending tape used by the librarian and the choir director is more versatile for many of their needs than the kind they now use. By adding their requirements to those of the other departments, the resulting quantity discount and lower number of requests might result in a significant over-all saving to the church.

Sometimes, of course, the purchasing agent will find that consolidation cannot be effected for all three using departments; the requirements of the secretarial personnel may be so heavy that the increased cost of the transparent mending tape could not be justified. In this case, consolidation of requirements would be made for only two of the three possible users.

THE RIGHT QUANTITY
AND THE RIGHT TIME

HOW MUCH IS ENOUGH

WHENEVER WE make a purchase of any kind, we decide what quantities we will buy. However, even in the area of personal choice, we do not have complete freedom to make this decision. Some aspects of the problem are inevitably decided for us by situations beyond our control. Take fuel, for example. If our buildings are heated by oil, the maximum quantity we can buy at any given time is decided for us by the amount that will fill our storage tanks to capacity. We do have some choice as to minimum quantity, and we will have something more to say about that part of the decision a little later in this chapter. If our church building is heated by gas, we have even less choice. The only way we can control the amount of gas we buy at any given time is by raising or lowering the thermostat. Even this gives us very little real choice, since the normal range of human comfort sets both an upper and lower limit to the thermostat setting. Beyond that limited range, we are completely at the mercy of outside elements.

We are indebted to A. L. McMillan[1] for a graphic ex-

[1] A. L. McMillan, *op. cit.*, p. 88.

ample of the problems of quantity and time that must be solved by the purchasing agent. Paraphrasing and adapting Mr. McMillan's example to our purposes, let us visualize the church administrator driving from his suburban New Jersey home to a workshop convention of his peers in some sunny Florida convention resort. On the way, good administrator that he is, he will make a number of stops to visit colleagues and to look over their operations to gain ideas for his own. Let us look at the purchase decisions he must make in buying gasoline during that trip. Conveniently for our illustration, our peripatetic administrator is traveling about 1,000 miles. He immediately knows that he will need about 60 gallons of gasoline. The buyer does not decide how much will be bought. He has a new car with a high compression engine and he wants top performance, so he will use premium grade gasoline—the specification is already decided for him. Whose brand of gasoline? He has a credit card from a major oil company, so he will use that and pay for the gasoline next month. Condition of the motor will determine somewhat how much gasoline will be used—that is a responsibility of the automotive mechanic. The exact route and extent of side-trips will affect the amount of gasoline; but that is a matter of his itinerary. There does not seem to be anything for the administrator to decide in the buying of the gasoline.

As he gets down to southern New Jersey, however, and approaches the Delaware River Bridge (100 miles), he realizes that there is a purchase decision coming up. He has used five to six gallons of gasoline and the tank has space for a purchase—should he fill it up? No, but as he drives along the question becomes more urgent. When does he buy and how much? If he stops for every five gallons, that would mean twelve stops and a big waste of time; if he can run until the tank is empty and then refill, that would mean only four stops and a great saving of time and convenience. But to try that might be embarrassing, expensive, and even dangerous. So he settles on a purchase of about twelve gallons, which means five stops.

Simple as this little story may be, it illustrates the basic problem of a church purchasing agent as he decides on the quantity and the timing for every transaction in which he is involved. Professional purchasing for the church is a great deal more complicated, of course. We cannot figure our requirements so easily at so much per mile. Our storage space is not limited to exactly so many gallons in a tank. Vendors do not always have all we want to buy—nor are they always at hand when we want a new supply. But generally, in a church, we buy, use, and then buy again. So it is not the total quantity to be purchased that concerns the buyer; it is the question of, "When do we buy and how much at a time?"

THE SMALL ORDER VERSUS THE LARGE ORDER

The most natural tendency for any relatively small organization with a limited budget is to buy on a hand-to-mouth basis. What could be more natural with a small budget than to nurse the limited funds from day to day. This solution is deceptively simple, and very expensive, in the long run. It is conceivable that there might be an emergency at the end of the fiscal year, as when a church without cash reserves finds itself dependent upon the weekly cash offering to meet its current expenses. Such situations might bring about a negative commentary on the church's over-all financial policy, but from a practical point of view it might necessitate hand-to-mouth buying for a limited period of time. However, an emergency expedient should never be a permanent practice. Continuous hand-to-mouth buying is inefficient. Instead of husbanding limited resources, it wastes them shamefully.

Does this mean that we never purchase small quantities, that we always buy every one of our needs in the largest possible quantity? Of course not. The large order obsession can be even more costly and wasteful of financial resources.

How then do we determine whether it is more advantageous to buy goods or materials with several transactions over a period of time than to acquire these items in single lots or under a single contract? On this matter, the question of relative costs comes into play. Businessmen in a profit-making enterprise try to subject each aspect of their operation to a careful cost analysis. The factor of costs must be considered very carefully when making purchasing decisions. In churches, the operational cost factors are more difficult to identitfy, and therefore are easier to ignore, but they are there and they are very real. Two principal costs are involved in purchasing for churches—the cost of storing goods and the cost of processing an order.

COSTS OF STORAGE

In profit-making enterprises, we calculate the economic value of space in terms of its potential productivity and other financial indicators. In a church, such standards are more difficult to identify and are frequently overlooked. After all, we have no profit-and-loss statement. Investment values of equipment and supplies are not ordinarily computed when preparing financial reports. Nothing is amortized for tax purposes. But there is probably no church in the world that has enough conveniently located storage space to satisfy all of its needs. Storage costs do exist in the church and they must be taken into account in administering the purchasing program.

Here is an example: The church has only one available empty storage closet. The business manager finds the church uses an average of 135 reams of mimeograph paper per year. However, in order to take advantage of a 100,000 sheet price break, he wishes to purchase 200 reams—an 18-month supply. This would save 30 cents a ream, or $60 —a net annual saving of $40. At the same time, the woman's society wishes to use the closet to store 500 glass punch cups that will be used twice a year. The net annual savings the women can achieve by buying rather than renting is only $20—half that obtained by buying mimeograph paper in large quantities. Thus, apart from the $60 capital cost of acquiring the cups, improper use of the limited storage space could cost the church $20 a year— the difference between the $40 annual saving on the large paper order and the $20 saving on cups. In actual practice, comparisons usually are less clear-cut, but such competing demands do exist in most churches. Even where there is no such competition for storage space, there are still identifiable costs for cleaning, lighting, heating, painting, and otherwise maintaining storage space.

COSTS OF PROCESSING AN ORDER

How can we identify and compute the costs of processing each order? Let us refer to page 21, where we listed the 17 basic elements of purchasing, starting with the anticipation of the need through the time required for placing purchased materials into service. Each of these actions is time-consuming, and each of them represents an assessable cost when performed by a paid employee. At the most conservative estimate possible—figuring the time of all employees involved at an average of $1.60 an hour, and assigning 10 minutes to each of these 17 operations—we come up with an average cost of over $4.50 for processing any order.

Staff personnel is always limited in a church, and the demand for jobs to be done is unlimited. Thus, in addition to the direct cost factor, we know that for every bit of time devoted to processing a purchase order for a routine item, that much less time is available for carrying on important program activities.

Returning to our example of the proposed purchase of mimeograph paper, we can see that if we buy a 3-month supply each time instead of an 18-month supply, we would be processing six times as many purchase orders at a cost of $24 over an 18-month period. On an annual basis, repeated small orders would cost us $18 a year, apart from the $40 annual price break of the 100,000 sheet purchase. Small-order purchasing here could add a needless $58 annual cost.

Small orders can be costly in terms of both time and money. But we can have problems with large orders as well. Here the problems are mainly related to the cost and inconveniences of finding adequate storage facilities and the need to tie up large amounts of operating funds in inventory. Let us look again at our mimeograph paper. If, instead of an 18-month quantity, we bought a 10-year supply at one time, the resultant quantity saving from a theoretical 1,000,000 sheet purchase might add an additional benefit of $20 a year. To store this large quantity, however, would require almost as much space as is required for a classroom. The cost of maintaining such a large supply room would be very great, probably outweighing any price differential. Moreover, by the time we come to the end of our 10-year supply, the quality of our mimeograph paper would have deteriorated tremendously.

Finally, during the 10-year period, we would have been tying up hundreds of dollars in inventory, instead of using these funds for essential program activities. Even if funds are available for such an extraordinarily large inventory, they would usually be better invested in a more liquid asset, with as much if not more financial reward. This example, of course, is an exaggerated one, but the principles involved are very real.

CONTROLLING THE SMALL ORDER PROBLEM

How can we control the small order problem? We must first realize that this problem exists. In many cases, part of the solution is found in a centralized purchasing system. We can cut down the cost of processing the small order by combining the requirements of several departments. We can reduce the cost further by making one purchasing transaction cover a number of different items. For example, we can assemble office supply requisitions from all departments at one time, one day a month, and avoid buying small quantities in between. We can also set up a central storage supply that will permit us to buy certain items in discount quantities and then charge them out to the using department in small lots. In doing this, however, we are increasing our inventory problems, the attendant paperwork, and, possibly, our storage costs.

Some churches solve the small order problem by increasing the use of the petty cash account, permitting various users to supply their needs directly through over-the-counter purchases at the retail level. Although this will solve some of the problems of repetitive purchases and save the cost of processing small orders, it can be a very dangerous practice if allowed to proliferate and get out of control. It is expensive partly because quantity discounts are impossible to realize and sales tax exemptions are often lost. Moreover, it loses all the other advantages of centralized purchasing.

OTHER FACTORS IN DETERMINING
PROPER QUANTITY

We have discussed in great detail two of the principal cost factors in determining the proper purchase quantity. Other costs also are important in a comprehensive purchasing program. Handling and transportation charges and quantity price differentials certainly have to be considered, but these actually are a part of the price of goods. As we have seen, the rate of return on invested funds might also influence our decisions as to whether to purchase in large or small quantities. However, cost factors are only some of the variables to consider in determining the proper quantity. Some of the other factors that will affect our decision are:

1. Quantity of stocks on hand.
2. Time and extent of probable use.
3. Commercial usage and practice.
4. Rate of deterioration or obsolescence.
5. Lead time required for delivery.

1. *Stocks on hand:* The amount of an item already on hand—the current inventory—will obviously have a great deal to do with the quantity of that item to be purchased. If the church nursery school submits a requisition for 6 gross of crayons, and our storeroom holds a 5-gross supply carried over from the preceding year, any wise purchaser will adjust the ordering quantity downward by a substantial portion of the 5 gross on hand. However, he would not deduct the entire 5 gross from the order; he would reserve a portion of the inventory—perhaps 2 gross—for an emergency cushion.

2. *Time and extent of probable use:* This refers to the period during which we will be using a needed item. Taking our crayons again as an example, if we used 10 gross a year, our 6-gross requisition at the beginning of the year might be increased. Another consideration is our rate of use. If we consume an average of 50 crayon pencils each and every week uniformly throughout the school year, then we might perhaps place several orders. On the other hand, if all the crayons are issued to all the teachers at the beginning of the year, the complete annual supply would have to be ordered prior to the beginning of the term, rather than phased out during the year.

3. *Commercial usage and practice:* Just as there is a theoretical ideal ordering quantity for any given item, so there is an ideal manufacturing and distributing quantity. In the manufacturing process, a certain amount of any material comes out of the machine during a given period. There are standard units of packaging also. Certain floor care items, such as wax and cleaning solvents, are generally packaged in 30- or 55-gallon drums. Smaller units for such items will generally be the 5-gallon can. These units will be the basis for formulating and quoting vendors' prices. It therefore becomes desirable for us, the consumer, to compute our requirements in similar standard units. The principle applies to many items and for this reason we buy mimeograph paper by the *ream;* light bulbs and paper towels by the *case.* In other cases, depending on the source, we may buy ritual candles by the *dozen* or by the *gross* or by the *pound.*

4. *Deterioration or obsolescence:* There can be no justification for purchasing any item in a quantity that cannot reasonably be expected to last beyond the point when it will continue to be in first-class condition. Paper and card stock will yellow with age and a good rule is never to order a supply of paper or envelopes that will last longer than 18

months. For some poorer qualities, such as newsprint or construction paper for classroom use, even 18 months is too long. Paint, wax, and many other commodities with perishable ingredients will deteriorate in time, as will ink, paste, and adhesive carrying items such as transparent tape.

5. *Lead time required for delivery:* This term has the ring of the large enterprise. It calls to mind the period required for putting a blast furnace into operation, setting up an atomic energy plant for the production of power or some other impressive and complicated activity. "Lead time," however, is basically a very simple concept. It is, for example, the period that elapses from the moment the maintenance superintendent decides that his stock of floor wax is getting low to the time the new drum is placed on its cradle in the basement with the dispensing spigot in place.

In other words, "lead time" is simply the period that elapses from the moment a need has been anticipated until the item has been placed in the hands of the user, ready for use. The purchaser needs time to anticipate a need and translate it into a completed purchase order. The manufacturer and distributor need time to make, assemble, package, and deliver the goods. The buyer, again, needs time to receive, inspect, adjust and deliver the goods to the using department. Lead time can vary from the twenty minutes needed by the landscape custodian to pick up a five-gallon can of gasoline for the lawn mower, to the two years or more required for design, manufacture, and installation of a new pipe organ.

THE USE OF FORMULAS

The "right" or "proper" quantity is a variable. Moreover, it is a subjective variable and there is plenty of room for difference of opinion about what the right quantity is in any given situation. Some have attempted to reduce the degree of variability through the use of a formula for making this decision. A 62-page booklet issued by the U.S. General Services Administration[2] boils down to a statement that the Economic Order Quantity (EOQ) is equal to 10 times the square root of the annual dollar requirement.

This formula is undoubtedly a fine one, and is relatively easy to use. For most churches, however, the decision as to the "right" quantity will continue to depend on the intelligent application of sound purchasing principles on a subjective basis. The wise buyer will make only minimal use of formulas for ". . . no formula can take the place of the purchasing department's judgment in individual cases."[3]

THE REQUIREMENTS CONTRACT

One of the most useful devices in church purchasing, which lets you have the big order "cake" while "eating it" on a small-order budget, is the so-called "Requirements Contract." Essentially, this is an open account or blanket order, under a firm price agreement. Such a contract can be either formal or informal. Under it, the amounts of our requirements generally are estimated and no definite quantity commitment is made to the vendor. However, both parties to the agreement have arranged that all the requirements of the church for the period specified will be acquired at a firm price from a single supplier. Such requirement contracts can be very useful for items used regularly by the church and which are regularly available on the market: linen supplies, cleaning supplies, office supplies, ritual supplies, candles, kitchen supplies. There

[2] *Economic Order Quantity*, U.S. Government Printing Office. Supt. of Documents, Washington, D.C. Stock No. 7610-543-6765; price, 35 cents.
[3] *The Handbook of the National Association of Church Purchasing Agents*, 1931, Volume I, p. 331.

usually is an option that deliveries under this agreement will be reasonably spaced throughout the period of the contract.

Obviously, such an arrangement can and should be made with only one supplier at a time for any particular item or class of items. In effect, what we have done when we establish a requirements contract is to arrange with a single vendor to carry an inventory from which we receive delivery as needed. Thus, we reduce lead time while acquiring some of the advantages of volume purchasing. Judicious use of the requirements contract can eliminate some of the hidden costs and inefficiencies inherent in repetitive small orders. Requirements contracts can also help reduce some of the disadvantages of the larger order, since in effect the buyer transfers to the supplier the costs of holding goods and of tying up capital. True, the supplier must pass on to us a proportionate share of the storage and capital costs, but he is a wholesaler who is amortizing these costs over a much larger volume than would be possible within the church itself.

Requirements contracts should be spelled out very carefully and specifically, and their provisions be fully understood by the buyer and the seller. For example, the vendor should clearly understand that the quantities mentioned in the original inquiry were estimates only and that while the church is not necessarily bound to the exact amount, it will probably order a quantity very close to this amount. At the same time, the church should realize that it has committed itself to buying those items included in the agreement only from the specified vendor, even if it should be able to acquire a temporary price advantage elsewhere during the period of the agreement. There has to be a clear understanding on the part of the vendor that, by his acceptance of the order, he is bound to deliver the goods as required and immediately upon demand, and that he is to maintain an inventory that is adequate to satisfy all reasonable requirements of the church.

GUIDELINES FOR QUALITY AND TIMING

In general, the following practices should be used as a guide in deciding the quantity and timing of church purchases:

1. Prepare a realistic yardstick for the minimum ordering quantity for any given class of commodity based on:
   a. Rate of use
   b. Stocks on hand
   c. Availability and costs of storage
   d. Commercially available quantities and packaging units
   e. Administrative costs of processing orders
   f. Lead time
   g. Deterioration and obsolescence
2. Consolidate requirements of all using departments for the same items in order to increase volume.
3. Purchase materials, as far as possible, in standard package and commercial lots.
4. Make purchases large enough to take advantage of quantity discounts, including all foreseeable needs on an annual basis or longer, where possible, but order no more than is necessary to obtain these price advantages for the designated operating period.
5. Use a blanket supply agreement or requirements contract wherever feasible to purchase items used in repetitive quantities on a regular basis.

Chapter 5

PURCHASING VALUE—
THE RIGHT QUALITY

WHAT IS THE RIGHT QUALITY

IN POPULAR PARLANCE, we talk about "quality" as if it were a single, readily definable characteristic. If the concept of quality were this definite, purchasing would be much simpler. Unfortunately, quality is a much more elusive concept. It is, at one and the same time, a combination of many varied elements. To complicate matters further, it is a variable combination of each of these elements. The final determination of the right quality is almost always a compromise achieved by assigning a relative weight to each of these variants.

A few of the variable factors that should be considered in determining the right quality are:

1. Durability
2. Productivity
3. Versatility
4. Dependability
5. Efficiency in operation
6. Ease and simplicity of operation
7. Ease and simplicity of repair
8. Convenience of service facilities

59

9. Time- and labor-saving features
10. Economy of operation and maintenance
11. Initial cost price
12. Availability on the market.

Note that in this listing we have placed price near the end. This is not because price is unimportant. The "right quality" is determined to some extent by price, but it is not measured by price alone. In arriving at the final determination of quality, price should be considered only after the other variables have been evaluated. Every careful buyer can vouch for the phenomenon that, in almost every field of supply we sometimes find almost identical items selling for prices that vary according to the market, the buyer, and the vendor. The cliché that "you get just what you pay for" is, all too often, not true, or at the best a half-truth.

Of the foregoing 12 variables that enter into the concept of the "right quality," the first 10 boil down to the general category of "suitability." This becomes the basic consideration, because from the buyer's point of view the best quality is, first of all, that which is best adapted to a particular need. Only after we have determined which of the competing products being considered are suitable according to this criterion can we proceed to consider the other factors: "cost" and "availability."

A product is not simply "good"; it should be "good for" a certain purpose, and the word "quality" takes on meaning only in relationship to that purpose. Thus, the right quality is not necessarily the highest quality. Sometimes the lowest quality is the proper choice. The product that will do the job properly should be the acceptable quality. An item that will not do the job properly is the wrong item regardless of price or how easy it was to acquire. On the other hand buying articles that are better than necessary is just as wasteful as buying items that are not good enough.

Thus, one of the most important functions of the church purchasing agent is to determine what the quality range should be for each purchase; to decide which of the varying levels of quality is most closely tied to our criterion of "suitability." He starts by establishing the minimum acceptable quality he considers to be necessary for the intended use. In most cases, the buyer will find that above this minimum quality a number of products are competing for his choice, but each of these will vary to some extent in the way their different quality components meet the over-all criterion of suitability.

When we move above the minimum acceptable quality, the second major determinant of the ideal—price (which we will consider in Chapter 6)—begins to enter the picture. The choice of the most suitable quality, at the price which is most fair and reasonable, combine to give us the most elusive and highly sought-after condition that we call the "best value." If this best value is available on the market at the time we want it, then we have satisfied all three basic criteria and we have the "right quality."

"Availability" is our next criterion. For this, we need to consider our sources of supply and the vendors we deal with. ("Availability" and sources of supply will be considered in Chapter 7.) Before we get to that, however, we have to know how we determine the right quality for our church and how we go about getting it.

WHO DETERMINES THE RIGHT QUALITY

The determination of quality is a joint responsibility of the church's purchasing agent and the using department. The degree of responsibility each has will vary among the various classifications of items that are bought and within each classification from time to time. It will also depend upon how specialized is the use to which the item will be put, and on the degree of specialized knowledge possessed by both the user and the purchasing agent. A high degree of cooperation is important in this area.

For specialized equipment and supplies, the general rule is that the user should have the major say in the determination of quality. The music director ordinarily is in a better position than the business manager of the church to determine the specifications required for music stands. If an extension ladder is being purchased, the building manager or head custodian may be the best judge of the maximum height to which an extension ladder should reach, as well as of attachments required to hold the supplies and equipment that will be used from this ladder.

However, the central purchasing agent need not and should not delegate all decision-making to the specialist. Even though he may not know all technical requirements of the article being purchased, his total purchasing experience will have given him a recognized professional competence in this field. He will know what questions should be asked, and he should preserve his prerogative of questioning any quality specification that appears to him unreasonable or even doubtful. The central purchasing agent usually is in the best position to pass judgment on items in common use throughout the church.

Cooperation is the key word, and conflicts as to who has the primary responsibility for determining quality should be very rare. The church purchasing agent can make an outstanding contribution by assembling adequate information on all items in general use throughout the church. A common grade of mimeograph paper, for example, will probably meet the needs equally well of the education department, the editor of the church bulletin, and the minister of music. It is important to remember, however, that, even for routine items, needs may vary according to specialized uses. For example, a typewriter for the secretary to the pastor may be used primarily for typing correspondence on fine engraved stationery. For this, a 13-inch carriage, a unique and dignified wide type face, a nonstandard ribbon color, and a soft platen may be highly desirable. On the other hand, a clerk-typist in the church business office may be better served by a 17-inch carriage for typing exacting financial reports, by a thin, elite standard type face for maximum sharpness in typing stencils, and by a hard platen for additional clarity in duplication.

Personal choice of the user should be a factor in any consideration of over-all quality. No matter how technically "right" the quality of an item might be when judged by all objective criteria available to a professional buyer, the lack of acceptance by the user might be a factor strong enough to make such a determination unsatisfactory. For many items, personal choices may be encouraged, since people work best, after all, when they are furnished with things they like to work with. Thus it was not surprising to us to read recently that the U.S. Government General Services Administration is planning to stock a variety of secretarial chairs in order to permit clerical workers to choose the type most suited to their individual requirements. Even in the largest church, it is unlikely that such a wide choice of furniture can be offered. Still, an article such as a chair, if constantly used by a valued church worker, can, with considerable justification, be purchased primarily on the basis of personal choice. The small church has the advantage over a large church when it comes to personal choice for purchase of new equipment. In a one-girl office, the secretary-typist can be given a great deal more freedom in selecting a typewriter than would be possible in a large church already possessing a battery of typewriters of the same brand. Here, the savings resulting from the use of common spare parts, supplies, and service contracts, might outweigh the desirability of moving to a new brand for an additional typewriter or for a replacement of one now in use.

Although the likes and dislikes of most individuals probably arise from the same underlying source as do those of the professional purchasing agent—namely, technical knowledge and past experience—these are also quite likely to be influenced by whim, caprice, or similarly subjective criteria that have no relationship to actual quality. We remember a custodian who objected arbitrarily to a new superior floor wax because he had been using a competing brand for a long time. It did not matter to him that the buyer had determined, on the basis of actual use comparisons, that the new wax spread with less effort, dried more quickly, stood up for a much longer period under a heavier traffic load, buffed to a good gloss after each use with the minimum of effort, retained its nonslip qualities throughout its life, and caused no injury to the floor itself —all at a cost some 15 per cent below that of the competing brand. The custodian maintained that he "just couldn't get used to the new wax" and that he "just knew it wasn't nearly as good." No amount of objective demonstration or rational discussion could persuade this custodian initially that his personal choice was unreasonable. He accepted the decision ultimately, not without a great deal of grumbling, which continued until he was furnished with a brand new buffing machine to replace an obsolete one and was given his personal choice from among two competing brands.

DESCRIBING THE RIGHT QUALITY

Once we have decided on the elements of quality that will make an item most suitable for our needs, we must decide how much weight to give to each of these elements and how to describe them to our suppliers. Suitability, as we have seen, is the product of different factors existing in varying combinations. For example, in furnishing the pastor's office, the element of color and style might rate first, efficiency of operation second, durability—while still important—might rank a little farther down the list. On the other hand, if we are buying filing cabinets for the business office, efficiency of operation would undoubtedly be a prime consideration, followed closely by durability. Color has only recently come to be a factor in selecting office furniture, as manufacturers have begun to offer alternatives to the standard drab office gray. Even so, color and style would weigh far less than those of durability and efficiency of operation.

Determining the quality elements to our satisfaction is only the first phase of quality determination. The next step is to provide our supplier with a description that will clearly depict the kind of article we want and its major characteristics. We must do this in a way that will insure that our prospective suppliers understand exactly what we wish. Here are some of the principal ways of expressing such a description:

1. *By brand name or catalogue designation.* This method is probably most familiar to nonprofessional purchasers. It is extremely simple, yet it is not, in every situation, the most satisfactory method of describing an article.

2. *By purchase specification.* This is the most precise way of describing to a prospective supplier the specific quality of items desired. It is also the most complicated and diffi-

cult method, and therefore has some inherent limitations for the church buyer.

3. *By blueprint.* As a graphic description of what is wanted, a blueprint presents a clear picture of the dimensions and relationships of the parts of one item with another. A blueprint is rarely used by itself. Most often, it is used in combination with specifications or other descriptive materials. It is most suitable for construction work and specially designed for heavy equipment. Otherwise, the blueprint is seldom used by the church purchasing agent.

4. *Market grade.* This measurement may be informal and commonly understood in the industry that markets the item in question or it may be officially promulgated (and in some cases policed) by trade associations, commodity market authorities, or Government agencies. Market grades are at best general descriptions covering a wide range of quality, but within this limitation they can be an adequate method of insuring consistency. For example, the church hostess, in requisitioning foodstuffs, would be well advised to take advantage of the U.S. Government grades and specifications for both fresh and processed foods. The maintenance supervisor will find that adherence to the common market grades of lumber is an easy way to insure consistency of size and quality of wood products he uses for the church. However, market grades are largely limited to bulk commodities that make up a small proportion of church purchases.

5. *By sample.* On its face, the use of a sample might be considered to be the most precise description of the item and its quality. In actual practice, however, the use of the sample for the product description will be of only occasional value. If, for example, we are buying C-fold paper towels and we know by experience that a certain combination of color, softness, and strength are most satisfactory,

we can order this quality by submitting a sample to prospective suppliers without going to all the trouble of determining the precise scientific specifications of this particular product. It is probable that the supplier can match the sample very closely, and that this matching can be established to the buyer's satisfaction by the use of testing. But adequate testing of the goods that are finally delivered is absolutely mandatory. Use of testing should be restricted to items in which the tangible or visible characteristics of size, color, and consistency can be readily determined by superficial inspection.

6. *By type and size.* This method of description is akin to the blueprint, in that its uses are limited to items that can be adequately characterized by a dimensional description. Hardware items, such as hand tools and nuts and bolts, are typical of the articles that can be described in this way. It should be recognized, however, that this method is really a variation of the detailed purchase specifications method in Number 2 above.

7. *By a combination of descriptive techniques.* In actual practice, the experienced buyer for a church will use a combination of the six methods noted above. But he will rely primarily on the first two: description by brand name, and description by purchase specification. Let us consider these in somewhat greater detail.

BRAND-NAME PURCHASING

The easiest way to describe the quality of an item is by the designation of a recognized brand name—a method that has several very important advantages. There is little chance of confusion when a brand name is specified, particularly when more descriptive information from the manufacturer's catalogue, such as model number, type, and catalogue number, is added. When we use a brand-name specification, we are taking advantage of considerable research and effort invested by the manufacturer in developing the specific item. A brand name is a manufacturer's treasured possession. It is the pillar upon which he has built his business reputation and upon which his hope for the future of his business rests. He is, therefore, very loathe to reduce the quality components below certain acceptable standards. By establishing such minimum standards, the producer renders a service to the purchaser.

Once we have demonstrated the suitability of a branded item, we can know, in most cases, without further research or investigation, that the item will continue to be suitable as long as we specify this particular brand name. True, a manufacturer may improve or otherwise change his product from time to time without changing the brand name, but generally he has too much tied up in his brand-name reputation to risk serious diminution of over-all quality. These characteristics of the brand-name product serve to create a ready user acceptance.

An important reason for purchasing equipment by brand name may be seen in the interchangeability of attachments, supplies, and repair parts when more than one item of a certain brand is acquired. Thus, if the church owns one stencil duplicator of a particular brand, and if it has performed satisfactorily, there are compelling reasons to purchase the same brand of stencil duplicator when two machines become necessary. Similarly, if the church secretarial staff is using three typewriters of a certain brand and if they have proven satisfactory, there will be advantages to specifying the same brand of typewriter when the time comes to add a fourth typewriter. Not only do we thereby promote consolidation of supply and service requirements, but we also insure interchangeability of skills. How often have we seen a clerk balk at using a substitute machine for the one she has been using because "it has a different feel," or because the controls are differently placed, or because she "doesn't know how to change the ribbon."

But the very reasons that suggest the use of the brand name, carry suggestions of the defects inherent in this type of specification. Branded products often are somewhat higher priced than unidentified items of the same or similar composition. We recognize a branded item we like as a "quality" item, and we expect it to be somewhat higher priced because of this sure-fire identification. The brand-name designation is also somewhat monopolistic. It tends to limit competition and the freedom of choice which the buyer theoretically should have.

Virtually every item we buy is available in a quality that is at least comparable from a variety of sources. When we limit our buying to brand-name items we restrict our selection of supply sources, and we are, in effect, eliminating a degree of competition.

Manufacturers' brand names are not the only kind of brand names with which we are concerned. In the category of branded merchandise, we are also concerned with those items sold by a jobber or distributor under his own "label." Generally, these "labeled" items are less reliable in terms of consistent quality components than are manufacturers' brand names. For one thing, the distributor has a smaller proportionate investment in advertising and has much more freedom than a national manufacturer to change the components of the item he issues under his "label."

One of the principal categories of goods frequently found under the distributor's label rather than a manufacturer's brand are liquid janitor supplies, including cleaning compounds and waxes. Other examples are fertilizers and calcium-chloride de-icers. Items of this nature are generally made up of comparatively simple chemical formulas. By virtue of their packaging and brand designation, they often commend premium prices without offering any particular advantage in quality standards over competing brands or unbranded materials purchased in bulk.

Some alleviation of the disadvantages of brand name purchasing, as outlined above, can be accomplished when the requisitioner adds the phrase, "or equal." Starting with the brand name specification received from the using department, the buyer will solicit quotations from appropriate vendors using the specification, "Brand X or its equal," and adding specifications for such factors as type, number, size, capacity, attachments, accessories, and any other details that would normally have had to be included in specifying a purchase from the manufacturer or distributor of Brand X. The chances are that he will receive a number of quotations, including some on Brand X and others on Brands Y or Z, which the vendors claim to be substantially equal in quality to Brand X. If he is lucky, the buyer may find that the lowest price offer is for Brand X. His research is then over. He knows that the using department will be satisfied at the same time that the buyer is successful in obtaining the "standard" item at minimum cost.

But suppose that Brand X is not the lowest price offer—that the lowest price, in fact, is offered by the distributor of Brand Z. The buyer is then faced with the difficult and often complicated task of determining whether Brand Z is, in fact, "equal" to Brand X. Although he can make this determination himself, he will, more than likely, call in the requisitioner or user and perhaps obtain some technical assistance as well. Initially, they will want to determine whether Brand Z has as much *capacity or capability* as Brand X; that it is as *safe;* that it can be delivered within the required *lead time;* and that it can be *supplied, serviced,* or *repaired* with reasonable efficiency. There are, of course, other considerations in connection with the adequacy of most items, and while Brand Z may be *equal* in all *principal* quality components, it is unlikely to be *identical.* Each branded article has its own special feature. It is the responsibility of the buyer to determine whether the special features of Brand X do in fact make it superior to Brand Z; at the very least, whether the lack of certain special features offered by Brand Z will seriously detract from the over-all quality of Brand X. To make this comparison, the buyer, in consultation with the user, should list the quality characteristics most important for the intended use of the item that is being purchased. Against this list, he should evaluate each of the competing offers, beginning with specified Brand X and then proceeding to Brand Z, the lowest price substitute. If Brand Z is found wanting, then a similar comparison should be made with Brand Y, if it, too, is below Brand X in price. If neither of the two proffered substitutes matches the basic quality characteristics that are necessary and that are found in Brand X, then Brand X will be the article of choice, even though it is the most costly. But we will know by that time we have made a valid quality comparison.

PURCHASE SPECIFICATIONS

The most accurate way of getting across to prospective suppliers the specific quality and kind of item you desire to purchase is to submit a detailed and precise purchase specification. We know how important it is that quality be carefully defined—that "high" or "poor" is not enough of a description. Since quality is actually the composite of those characteristics or properties inherent in the material or product, we must find some way of measuring, defining, and describing each of the significant factors, so that we may know exactly what we want the supplier to furnish; so that the supplier can gauge exactly what he is expected to supply; and so that we, in turn, can measure the item against a mutually understood yardstick.

In a sense, any description of the item we are buying is a specification, whether we use a market guide, a national standard, a special description, or a brand name. The important thing is that the specification be adequate so that both we and the seller understand exactly what is to be delivered, when, where, how, and at what price.

The ideal purchase specification is drawn tightly enough to assure the church that it will receive the desired quality without sacrificing any important characteristics and without adding unnecessary features that will only add cost to the item. At the same time, it must be drawn loosely enough to insure that more than one supplier will have an opportunity to bid, so that there will be an adequate range of competition. All too often, a using department will request a specification so tightly drawn that only one supplier or brand name can meet the standards. Sometimes, these are based on personal choice. The buyer will often defer to the using department and purchase the desired quality even though he has reservations. But it is extremely important that everyone in the purchasing process be aware of the fact that unnecessarily tight specifications usually mean higher costs.

Though the purchase specification is a very accurate and precise technique for describing a need, it is not necessarily the most desirable one. For most purchases, the church purchasing agent will do as well to rely on brand

names, catalogue descriptions, samples, and other devices
we have discussed above. For one thing, it is impossible
to reduce all requirements for the average choice to
specific descriptive terms. Most of the items bought by
a church are small, both quantitatively and monetarily,
and the costs of preparing detailed purchase specifications
may be completely out of proportion to their value. The
occasions when the purchase specification is called for is
when we are buying items that have a very high intrinsic
value, or when the operating problems to be solved are of
a crucial nature. Thus the detailed purchase specification
is a highly important, desirable device in creating a new
pipe organ. Similarly, a detailed specification for floor wax
may be in order where a peculiar combination of climatic
conditions and flooring made from an unusually slick variety of lumber combine to present a peculiar hazardous
slippage problem on the social hall floor. In such cases, the
purchase specification is virtually essential to obtain the
desired quality and characteristics. It becomes necessary
at these times for the purchasing agent to be or to become
thoroughly conversant with the particular items or materials for which he is specifying. Also, this will insure that
the church does not receive a poorer or different quality
than was intended. It is important to realize that when the
purchaser draws up his own specification and the supplier
follows these exactly, the purchaser himself has assumed
complete responsibility for the quality and performance
of the product he has described.

When preparing detailed purchase specifications, the
buyer sets up the requirements in one or more of the following terms:

1. *Composition:* This is particularly well suited to the purchase of items that are identifiable by their chemical or

physical components, such as lawn fertilizer, floor wax, and de-icing compounds.

2. *Physical dimensions and measurements:* This type of description, often accompanied by a blueprint or dimension sheet, is a preferred way of describing improvements of the church building, construction of an organ, and fashioning of audio-visual display materials.

3. *Performance:* This specification describes the item being purchased by specifying exactly how it is to meet the needs of the church. Specifying a 16-mm motion picture projector that will throw an incandescent beam at least 80 feet with clarity in a room from which 80 per cent of outside daylight has been excluded" is this type of a performance specification.

4. *Method of manufacture:* This specification device should be used only where the church has very special requirements, because when we order on this basis, we must be prepared to accept the principal responsibility for the performance and quality of the designated item.

5. *Standard specification:* Frequently, the church purchasing agent can profitably use any of the wide variety of specifications already drawn up by trade associations, professional groups, and Government agencies.

INSURING QUALITY—VALUE ANALYSIS: INSPECTION

In church purchasing, value analysis is a technique based on the theory that the value of any part, material, or service should be determined by the task it performs. Thus, when we buy floor wax or paint, we are buying protection of floor or wall surfaces. The value of this wax or paint would be determined by the area of surface covered per dollar, after equating its permanence and related characteristics with those of competing products.

The technique of value analysis is important for everyone concerned with purchasing, whether for a small church or a large one. All purchasing for churches should be done in the light of an established discipline of examining each item from the point of view of its "function" as well as its material components.

A second procedure of quality determination and control, essential for every church, is the inspection of purchased goods, at the time they are received. This involves more than the simple identification of merchandise, particularly when new products are ordered and received for the first time. It includes mutual verification by testing and close examination in order to make certain that the quality specified has actually been delivered.

WARRANTIES

A seller, in order to effect a sale, may make a promise that an article, such as a piece of office equipment, will function in a specified manner, or he may represent the quality of an article in such a way as to cause the buyer to act on this representation. Such a promise or representation is a *warranty*. A warranty that is definitely stated or expressed by the seller is an *express warranty*. It is not necessary to use the word "warranty" or "guarantee" to create a warranty. Any words or expressions that indicate an intent to warrant the goods are sufficient.

When a seller makes statements of facts regarding goods, upon which the buyer relies, the seller must make good these representations. However, they must be statements of fact and not merely personal opinions or judgments. A salesman will talk up the value of the goods he is selling. Such statements as "the best for the money," "you can't beat this material at any price," and "our goods are superior to those of competitors" are known as sellers' talk or puffing. They are not warranties. If the buyer wants to be sure that the goods ordered will be satisfactory, he should obtain protection by requiring an express warranty. He may ask for: (1) a definite representation concerning the quality or capacity of the goods; or (2) a statement that the article will be of a certain kind or will perform in a specified manner.

Implied warranties: Even though the seller makes no promise or representations, certain warranty obligations are ascribed to him by law. These are called *implied warranties*. These are voided when certain express warranties interfere or when the parties agree to the avoidance: for example, when the seller sells goods "as is."

In order to protect the buyer of goods, the seller is required by law to "warrant" that he has the right to sell the goods and that the buyer will have good title and undisturbed possession of them. A buyer may inform the seller as to the purpose for which the goods are required. The buyer does this in reliance on the good judgment and skill of the seller in choosing the goods. In this case, the law requires that the seller select goods that are reasonably fit for the use to which the buyer wishes to put them. The basis for the warranty that the goods shall be suitable for their intended uses is the reliance by the buyer on the good judgment and skill of the seller. There is no warranty that the goods are suitable for a particular purpose when the buyer himself selects the goods or when he orders goods according to certain specifications or under a special trade name.

Where there is a sale of goods by description, the law requires the seller to warrant that the goods fit the description. Labels and descriptions on packages must truthfully describe the contents of the package. Also, when goods are sold under a trade name, the seller warrants that the quality of the goods conforms to that ordinarily associated with that trade name. In a sale by sample, the seller impliedly warrants that the goods will conform to the sample. When goods are sold by a manufacturer or by a wholesaler or retailer who commonly handles such goods, the law generally implies a warranty that the goods are merchantable. In the case of a purchase by a church, this means that the goods shall be suited for the use to which goods of this kind are ordinarily put.

Caveat emptor: When a buyer has the opportunity to inspect goods before purchasing them and does so, the seller, in the absence of fraud, is relieved of such responsibility. In this case, the buyer may not complain about defects in the goods that he could have ascertained by ordinary inspection. It is really the buyer's duty to examine and test the goods before he makes a purchase. If he fails to do so, and gets the worst of the bargain due to his own carelessness and failure to examine the goods, he must shoulder the blame himself. The rule applies the maxim, *caveat emptor*, a Latin phrase meaning "Let the buyer beware." This is a principle carried down from the English common law. If a buyer does not wish to rely on his own knowledge and judgment, he may protect himself by requiring that the seller make an express warranty against defects.

Chapter 6

PURCHASING VALUE—PRICE

THE ROLE OF PRICE

IN THE PRECEDING chapter, we explored ways of determining and obtaining the proper quality. This is so we can help insure that we are receiving the utmost value for each purchasing dollar.

But quality is only one face of the value coin. The other side—and just as important—is price. As servants of the Lord, we know that money is a very inadequate measure of the important values in life. From an economic standpoint, however, money is an indispensable measuring device. We must use it to arrive at any meaningful determination of economic value.

Value is a measure of the desirability of an article or service acquired for the church. *Price* is value expressed in money.

One outstanding authority on purchasing offers the following formula:

$$\text{VALUE} = \text{QUALITY} \div \text{Price}[1]$$

[1] Stuart F. Heinritz, *Purchasing: Principles and Application,* 3rd ed. (Englewood Cliffs, N.J.: Prentice-Hall, Inc., 1959), p. 204.

This is a symbolic way of expressing the general principle that both quality and price contribute to the determination of value. Restated, this formula means that value varies *directly* in proportion to the quality received and *inversely* in proportion to the price paid.

In Chapter 5, we saw how important it is for the church purchasing agent to obtain proper quality, and that frequently the price may be relatively unimportant in an over-all value sense. But let's face it. Regardless of how unimportant price may be in terms of over-all value, price can never be ignored, inasmuch as the church's business is everyone's business. Quality and durability, in many cases, may be the dominant factors, and in those cases the church purchasing agent may make purchase decisions primarily in terms of these factors. Nevertheless, he must be prepared to justify his purchase on a relative price basis, because this is the way it will be evaluated by the governing board at the church.

Buying things at the lowest practicable prices simplifies other aspects of management. The lower the prices, the more things we will be able to buy; the more desires we will satisfy, the more facets of the church program we will be able to support.

In the final analysis, then, the price the church pays is as much a factor in the final decision of what is "the best buy" as are the technical properties of the product.

WHAT IS A PROPER PRICE

From the church buyer's point of view, the purchase is not successful unless the price is "fair and reasonable."

"Fair and reasonable?" From whose point of view? The buyer's, or the seller's? We know the answer to that question. The price has to be fair and reasonable to the church on whose behalf we are exercising our purchasing judg-

ment. But the seller is also seeking to determine a fair and
reasonable price from his point of view. Both the buyer
and the seller come together in the market place seeking a
price that is fair and reasonable to both. Out of this meeting of minds comes what we call the "fair market price."

The proper price—the fair and reasonable price—is one
that bears some reasonable relationship to the service rendered by the article we are buying. It must be a competitive price. That is, it must be no higher than the price
charged by the vendor under similar circumstances, and it
must be at least as low as we would have to pay for comparable goods or services from any other supplier. Finally,
it must be a price the church can afford to pay. What do
we mean by the phrase, "afford to pay"? In the commercial
world, "afford to pay" means a price which, when added
to all other costs, will leave a profit when the finished
product is sold.

For the church administrator, the term "afford to pay"
refers to his ability to allocate a portion of the financial
resources of the church to the purchase of specific goods
or services.

FACTORS AFFECTING "MARKET PRICE"

As buyers, we are not officially concerned with the manner in which the seller determines his selling price. As long
as the price is fair and reasonable and one we can afford
to pay, we have no formal interest in how it is set. However, the professional buyer wishes to know *why* prices
change and what factors go into establishment of price.
This is so that he can make a better judgment as to the
fairness and reasonableness of the price he is offered. He
wants to know these things not only so as to judge the
present price, but also in order to forecast future price
trends.

Economists tell us that there are three main determinants of market price: (1) costs of production and distribution, (2) supply and demand, and (3) competition. The first of these—costs—sets the lower limits of the market price over a sustained period of time. The manufacturer and the distributor—if they are to earn a profit—must take home a sum that will more than cover costs of raw materials, manufacturing, distribution, and overhead. These matters are not of direct concern to us as purchasing agents, though we should be aware of them. We are, however, directly concerned with the market conditions of *supply* and *demand* and *competition*. Let us examine these concepts more closely.

SUPPLY, DEMAND, AND COMPETITION

In a completely free market, the "natural" law of supply and demand would tend to keep supply, demand, and price—in balance. However, prices of most items the church buys do not fluctuate in a completely free market. Many of the manufactured goods bought by the church are sold at so-called "administered" prices. The price here is frequently held constant. However, as the demand (as determined by sales volume) tends to increase at the administered price level, the manufacturer will change his production schedule to increase the supply or administer the price upward. As sales demand drops, the supply is artificially reduced by curtailment of production schedules in order to maintain the price.

However, under our free enterprise system the market is still affected by supply and demand and often responds to changing conditions by giving rise to *sellers' markets* and buyers' markets. In the sellers' markets, supplies are short, prices are higher, discounts are withdrawn, price lists are revised upwards, salesmen are scarce, and competition for available business declines. On the other hand, during a *buyers' market,* suppliers compete more actively for the church's business. Suppliers are ample, prices tend to be lower, attractive discounts are offered, many salesmen call on the church, and offer "bargains" and additional services.

PURCHASING FOR THE CHURCH
IN THE COMPETITIVE MARKET

To a greater or lesser degree, the competitive market creates the "market value" which sets the range of prices we expect to pay. As good purchasers, we would be derelict in our duty if we paid more. We cannot realistically expect to pay less. But within this range, there frequently is room for negotiation by both the buyer and seller. Our task as church purchasing agents, therefore, is to discover the fair and reasonable market price range, and then to act on it in the best interests of our congregation.

The church purchaser can do very little to change the over-all market situation in any given economic period, but his knowledge and experience can help to protect his church's interests when fluctuations occur in the market. During a sellers' market, the church purchasing agent refuses to accept without question the extreme high prices he is faced with. He combs the market for alternative suppliers and substitute products, and he opens his share of the market to competitive sellers and their products. In a buyers' market, he looks for the most favorable prices obtainable in the lower market range, and he assures himself of these prices through long-term supply contracts, thus stabilizing the market for his church for a long period ahead.

GOVERNMENT AND THE
COMPETITIVE MARKET

Numerous Governmental regulations, though not directed at the church purchasing agent, affect the market in which he buys, and he should know about them. The Sherman Act, the McGuire Act, the Clayton Act, the Federal Trade Commission Act, and the Wheeler-Lea Act are among the Federal laws that tend to keep the market freer. These acts concern themselves with matters of monopoly, conspiracy in the restraint of trade, and false and misleading advertising.

Fair trade laws, such as the Robinson-Patman Act, the Miller-Tydings Act, and various state laws modeled on them, work in the opposite direction: to restrict price freedom. These laws grew out of the great depression of the 1930's, when prices plummeted and remained low for a long time. Churches and nonprofit institutions are specifically excluded from the provisions of these laws and recent court decisions have placed various curbs on their applicability to other consumers. Nevertheless their effect is often far-reaching, and they influence in many ways the market within which the church purchasing agent moves.

DISCOUNTS

Prices may be quoted to the church buyer at either a "net" unit price or a "list" price. The unit price designation is clear and simple. The purchaser knows that this is the price he will actually pay. The term "list price," however, is a suggested retail price the church buyer may *not* have to pay. It is a price set by the manufacturer or the distributor at the level at which he would *like* the goods to be sold to the ultimate consumer. In practice, the list

price is the starting point from which further price deter-
minations are made. When the church purchaser hears
that the phrase "list price" is "X dollars," his typical reply
is, "What is my discount?"

Numerous types of discounts are prevalent in the open
market. Many of these, such as "chain discounts," are
highly technical and relate primarily to industrial and
commercial buyers who purchase in large quantities and
at several distributive levels. The ones that affect the
church buyer most intimately are *quantity discounts, trade
or church discounts, and cash discounts.* Let us consider
each of these discount categories separately.

Quantity Discounts: The responsibility for obtaining
discounts—or discounts for volume—rests with the buyer.
Manufacturers and distributors reduce the per-unit costs
of most items as the purchase volume goes up. In part, this
is because manufacturing, distributing, and handling costs
are reduced as larger volumes are handled at one time. Frequently, however, quantity discounts are available even
when these unit costs are relatively stable. This is because
volume business is more attractive to a vendor. Administrative costs of volume sales are always relatively lower,
since paperwork and negotiation is reduced. Therefore,
vendors are usually willing to compete actively for volume
business. Even when quantity discounts are not openly
offered by vendors, the purchaser can frequently invite
them by asking for quotations on various items at varying
levels of demand.

Of course, large quantity purchases are not always justified, even where attractive discounts for volume are
available. In Chapter 4, we learned how storage facilities,
depreciation, obsolescence, and related factors can affect
quantity determination. Nevertheless, it is important to
note that if smaller orders for goods are placed individually,

without reference to total annual demand, the possibility of quantity discounts is often overlooked. When purchases are made on an open account or a requirements contract, we may not always be able to determine in advance just what the total volume will be. However, we do have the opportunity of reviewing the account periodically and of taking future advantage of volume discounts based on our purchase experience over a long period of time.

Trade Discounts: Here the discount is granted on a graduated scale according to the supplier's classification to his customers. Trade discounts are not necessarily related to the size of the order (although in some cases they do incorporate volume discounts); instead, they are primarily tied to a distributor's marketing system. Trade discounts are not necessarily discriminatory. They do reflect the vendor's awareness that a particular category of customer is a valuable and desirable one and that his business should be sought.

A so-called "church" discount is in the category of a trade discount. Some people claim that when a church purchaser seeks a church discount, he is demeaning the institution and engaging in unethical and discriminatory haggling. It is our own belief that nothing could be further from the truth. The church purchaser should never hesitate to ask for a special church discount. He is failing to play fair to his employer when he neglects or hesitates to ask for such price advantages. Many firms have a policy of making contributions through discounts to churches, and we should no more discourage giving in this area than we would discourage public contributions of other types. The same is true for "educational discounts" for materials purchased for the church school.

On the other hand, churches have certain responsibilities regarding the acceptance of such discounts. They must never be accepted under false pretenses for the benefit of individuals nor for uses that are not entitled to such special discounts.

Cash Discounts: Custom dictates that churches, in common with other purchasers, pay their bills within 30 days. Many vendors, in order to increase their operating capital, will offer an additional inducement for earlier payment— i.e., "two per cent discount for payment within ten days."

From the supplier's point of view, a cash discount is not a price concession; it is an inducement offered to the buyer to pay quickly. The church buyer has a distinct obligation in connection with cash discounts. He must never assume that such a discount is granted unless it has been promised or unless he has clearly stated his expectations on his purchase order and the vendor has failed to refuse his request. The church reaps an additional advantage from regular use of cash discounts; when the church discounts its invoices regularly and on time it enjoys a better credit rating. This is always a big help to successful buying.

Many churches pay their bills twice a month. For example, they may pay invoices that have arrived in the last half of the month on the fifth day of the succeeding month, while all invoices which have arrived during the first half of the month are paid on the twentieth. Where such regular payment dates exist, and if we wish the cash discount to apply to payments made on such a date, we should have a firm understanding with our vendors, preferably in writing.

TAXES

Taxes are another cost factor of price. Transportation taxes generally do not greatly affect the price of items that churches buy. Neither do payroll taxes, except when the church buys services on a contract basis. In such cases, social security and other payroll taxes must be considered when comparing the cost to the church of performing the services with its own labor, or contracting for the services of an outside organization.

Churches are usually excused from state and local sales and use taxes, but Federal excise taxes must generally be included as part of the total cost of office equipment and maintenance equipment purchased for general church use. However, where an item subject to excise tax is purchased for strictly educational use, Federal excise terms may be deducted. Examples are excise taxes on communication and travel that are exclusively for the church school. Some churches have one or more of their trunk telephone lines terminate in the school office, and are thus entitled to deduct the Federal excise tax from this bill. Where the volume of telephone traffice justifies such an arrangement, the local telephone company business office will probably be happy to work with the church business manager in preparing the necessary forms.

OTHER INFLUENCES ON PRICE

Freight is a cost factor that affects price, particularly on heavy equipment. So is the *availability of service* to equipment and the ultimate cost of such service. The inability to obtain adequate preventive maintenance or service could easily increase the cost of an item far beyond what was initially expected. For example, if an office machine is to be placed under a service agreement at the expiration of the guarantee period, the cost of such service agreement must be considered in the purchase price. It is conceivable that service costs may send the ultimate price much higher than the buyer had initially planned. Consider the purchase of an adding machine at an initial cost of $150. It was chosen over a similar machine of approximately equal quality which had a $170 initial cost. The annual service contract price for the cheaper machine is $20; for the second machine, it is $15. Over a 10-year period, the combined initial and service cost of the adding machine with the higher initial price will be only $320, compared to $350 for the "cheaper" machine—a saving of over 10 per cent. On a 15-year life expectancy, there will be a total comparative saving of $55, or more than one-third of the initial purchase price of the $150 machine.

Installation charges can sometimes become a significant expense factor of final cost; this should be considered very carefully before any equipment is purchased. Attention should also be paid to the *guarantee* or *warranty* on equipment items.

QUALITY AND PRICE

We return to quality, the other major element of our value equation shown on page 78. What weight shall be given to quality when seeking to determine the fair and reasonable price of an item to be purchased by the church?

In some situations, the lowest quality at the lowest price is the appropriate combination. In others, only the highest quality can be justified, even if the highest quality entails the most expensive price. Take the matter of lawn mowers. Church A, in the suburbs, has an extensive lawn that is mowed by the regular maintenance personnel, each of whom is mechanically inclined and is a highly responsible individual. For this congregation, a high-quality, strong, estate-type mower is the most appropriate purchase, because the durability and long life of this equipment can be protected over a long period of time, particularly with a service contract.

Church B, on the other hand, has a tiny lawn in its downtown location. Its lawn mower is used only sporadically by inexperienced, part-time help. For Church B, an inexpensive promotional-type mower, which can be bought at any supermarket or hardware store for less than $50, might be the most appropriate buy.

Chapter 7

PURCHASING VALUE— SELECTING OUR SOURCES AND PLACING THE ORDER

AVAILABILITY

EVERY TIME we go to the automobile show, we are treated to a view of the "car of the future." It is a beautiful creation, loaded with features that add to the comfort, safety, and prestige of the owner. It is made of the best quality materials, with the highest degree of craftsmanship. One glance at this magnificent vehicle establishes the desire and hypnotizes us into feeling a need for acquiring this lovely conveyance. The only trouble with it is that it is not available. The quality of an item may conform to our exact specifications, and the price may be right, but before we can begin to purchase it we must establish its *availability*.

By "availability," we do not mean merely that the article we seek can be found and purchased somewhere, sometime, or somehow, or, if it cannot be found on the open market, that it can be fabricated. From a practical point of view, we have not only to be able to buy some of it now, but we have to be able to buy enough of it to satisfy all of our needs over the full period we will be needing it. We should also be able to purchase from "alternative sources"—to make a choice from several vendors.

How do we discover the availability and the sources of supply? By what factors should we be guided in choosing a vendor? In what manner should we work with vendors over a period of time, and in what way should we negotiate with them to purchase goods and services in the right quantity, at the right time, of the proper quality, and at the right price?

KINDS OF SUPPLIERS

Before the buyer can select the appropriate vendor he has to decide at which level of the marketing process he will be operating: the "wholesale level," the "jobber level," or the "retail level."

Wholesale Purchasing: It is an axiom of purchasing that the closer we get to the original source of supply, the lower will be the price. The manufacturer, of course, is the ultimate source, but most churches do not purchase in quantities to which the manufacturer is accustomed. The manufacturer generally will refer a church buyer to a "wholesaler" or "manufacturer's representative." The wholesaler does not usually provide any personalized service to his customer. His function is to procure large lots from the manufacturer and break them into smaller units. Usually, however, these wholesale units are still too large to serve the church regularly, yet in some instances the church can profitably deal with a wholesaler. A purchase of duplicating paper in quantities to last for a year or more is one example. Also, a church seeking to buy several hundred folding chairs for the church assembly hall usually can go directly to the wholesale distributor or to the "manufacturer's representatives."

Buying from a Jobber: Most often, the church buyer looks to the "jobber" for quantity purchases. By whatever title the jobber is known: "dealer," "supplier," "distributor," or "outlet"—he generally carries substantial stocks and makes his sales in smaller packages than does the wholesaler, or in broken lots, such as half-cases. Like the wholesaler, the jobber generally does not render personalized service. However, for substantial quantities, he is a logical source, since his deliveries are reasonably prompt and because his prices generally are lower than those of retail establishments.

Buying at Retail: The "retailer" is the vendor with whom individual consumers usually deal. Amounts involved in each transaction generally are relatively small, but personalized service, opportunities for adjustment, trials, consultations, and small-lot deliveries ordinarily are available on short notice. The church buyer will usually try to get a more attractive price than the retailer quotes to the casual customer, but on many occasions the quantity sought can be economically acquired only from a retailer. Often, too, when a retailer can expect from a church a guaranteed market for quantities of goods it buys frequently and regularly, he will adjust prices appropriately. Sometimes an attractive requirements contract can be worked out with a retail supplier so that, in effect, he will provide the storehouse for goods we require frequently and consistently.

SOURCES OF INFORMATION ABOUT SUPPLIERS

There are 9 principal sources from which the church purchasing agent can obtain information about sources of supply for various goods and services and about individual vendors. These are:

1. *Experience and Memory:* These are highly subjective sources. The ability to draw upon past events and to apply lessons learned in former experiences to situations that

confront us now or in the future, is one of the hallmarks of wisdom in any area. This ability to draw upon past experience and memory of past events is usually the difference between the "seasoned" purchasing agent and his "green" counterpart.

2. *The Vendor File:* This is simply an extension of a purchasing agent's memory. By keeping a listing, classified by each major area of purchasing activity (office supplies, maintenance supplies, gardening equipment, ritual objects), the buyer reinforces his spontaneous recall by recording his experiences with previous suppliers. This can form a ready reference when future needs arise.

3. *Source Books:* In addition to books on church management such as this one, a basic library should include some of the four volumes listed below. Each of them is a college level textbook. Although they all are geared to the purchasing problems and techniques of large profit-making organizations, they contain useful information for anyone engaged in purchasing.

England, Wilber B., *Procurement: Principles and Cases* (4th Edition). Homewood, Illinois: Richard D. Irwin, Inc., 1962.

Heinritz, S. F. *Purchasing: Principals and Applications* (4th Edition) Englewood Cliffs, N.J.: Prentice-Hall, Inc., 1962.

Hodges, Henry G.: *Procurement: The Modern Science of Purchasing*, New York: Harper and Row, Publishers, 1961.

McMillan, A. L.: *The Art of Purchasing.* New York: Exposition Press, 1959.

Ritterskamp, Jr., James J., Abbott, Forest L., and Ahrens, Bert C.: *Purchasing for Educational Institutions,* Bureau of Publications, Teachers College, Columbia University, New York, 1961. This volume is specifically directed at the needs of large colleges and universities. Although the purchasing problems it discusses differ markedly from those of a church, there are many similarities because of the nonprofit nature of both types of organizations.

Aljian, George W. (Ed.) *Purchasing Handbook*, McGraw-Hill, New York, 1958. The emphasis in this voluminous and detailed source book is on the purchasing problems of giant industrial and commercial organizations. There is, nevertheless, much useful data and some helpful guides for all persons engaged in purchasing, whether for large or small organizations.

4. *Magazines and Trade Journals:* These can provide excellent sources of information about vendors, both in the text and in the advertisements.

The Office Magazine (published monthly by Office Publications, Inc., 73 Southfield Ave., Stanford, Connecticut)

Administrative Management (published monthly by Geyer-McAllister Publications, 212 Fifth Ave., New York, N.Y.)

Catholic Building Maintenance (published bimonthly by Joseph F. Wagner, Inc., 53 Park Place, New York, N.Y.)

Church Management (published monthly at 13308 Euclid Ave., Cleveland, Ohio 44112)

Protestant Church Building and Equipment (published four times a year by Ford Stewart, 27 E. 39th St., New York, N.Y.)

Your Church (published by The Religious Publishing Co., 122 Old York Rd., Jenkintown, Pa.)

In addition, specialized bulletins and publications issues by various denominational groups can be helpful. *Synagogue Service,* published for Reform Jewish congregations by the Union of American Hebrew Congregations, 838 Fifth Ave., New York, N.Y. is an example.

Large churches may also find it to their advantage to

subscribe to such specialized *purchasing magazines* as:

Purchasing, Conover-Mast Publications, Inc., New York, N.Y.

Purchasing Week, McGraw-Hill Publishing Co., Inc., New York, N.Y.

5. *Trade Directories:* Some of these directories that may be of occasional use to the buyer are:

Thomas's Register of American Manufacturers, Thomas Publishing Co., 461 Eighth Ave., New York, N.Y. This includes a trade-name section, cross-references byproducts, and an alphabetical section of leading manufacturers, their officers and officials, and other pertinent information.

Purchasing Directory: A single-volume published semiannually by Industrial Directories, Inc., Conover-Mast, 205 E. 42nd St., New York 17, N.Y.

MacRae's Bluebook, MacRae's Bluebook Co., 18 E. Huron St., Chicago 11, Illinois. A two-volume guide that has a classified material section, an index to advertisers and an address and trade name section.

6. *The Classified Telephone Directory:* This is a must in the library of every purchasing officer. Properly used it can be a great time saver and give much needed information to the alert purchasing agent. The more esoteric books and magazines listed above are available in many public libraries and can be especially useful to church buyers when looking for specialized items of equipment and service.

7. *Catalogs:* These are a basic element in any purchasing library. Even the smallest church can usually fill two or three shelf boxes with current catalogs of suppliers of most products used by the church. In the larger church, these catalogs will be more voluminous, and will be indexed

under such headings as "Cleaning Supplies," "Floor Maintenance," "Office Equipment and Supplies," "Furniture," and "Ritual and Ceremonial Objects."

8. *Direct Mail Advertising:* Such material is a frequent source of information about new products and new developments of particular interest to buyers.

9. *Interviews with Salesmen:* Too often, the salesman is looked upon in a purely negative light—as an intruder and a time-waster. However, he can be the church purchasing agent's greatest ally and one of the most fruitful sources of information about merchandise and market trends.

CRITERIA FOR CHOOSING SUPPLIERS

The foregoing sources of information about vendors are preliminary to the actual task of vendor selection. A basic question is: "How many vendors should our church use for a single category of goods?" On the one hand, we would like to have the largest possible purchasing volume so that our orders will be large and thus keep prices attractively low. Our internal costs also go down when we order in large volume, because there are fewer purchase orders to issue and follow up. However, if we concentrate all of our purchasing of a major item (such as mimeograph paper) in a single vendor, we leave ourselves pretty much at his mercy, and we lose all of the advantages of a competitive market. Accordingly, it is sometimes an excellent idea to distribute at least some of our major volume purchases among two or even three different suppliers. In this way, we protect the continuity of our supply even if one of the vendors should be unable or unwilling for some reason to take care of our needs.

Most churches have established an historical record of

vendors to whom they habitually give their business. Sound purchasing practice does not require us to scrap for trivial reasons our arrangements with vendors who have been serving us satisfactorily over a period of time. There may be no incentive to make changes, except where new products or new methods come into the picture, or where we have reason to believe that we are paying more than a fair and reasonable price for the materials and services we buy regularly.

Sometimes our regular vendors will cease to be available to us because they have gone out of business or for some other reason are unable to meet our needs. At other times, we will become dissatisfied with one of our regular suppliers—perhaps because prices have risen too rapidly or too frequently, or because his service or the quality of his merchandise has deteriorated. At still other times, we will be in the market for goods or services we have never purchased before and for which we have to seek a new supplier.

Whatever the reason for our seeking a new vendor, we need a checklist of criteria to help us make a sound appraisal. Here are some characteristics of a good supplier:

1. *Price:* His goods and services are available at fair and reasonable prices.
2. *Quality:* His goods and services meet our standards, and the quality is consistent for all items furnished.
3. *Capacity:* He has adequate facilities, knowledge, capability, and inventory for supplying our total needs and for providing any service or follow-up necessary after the merchandise is delivered.
4. *Management:* His financial position is secure enough to assure us that he can fulfill his commitments to the church over a long period of time; his management practices are progressive and alert so that we are always given the

latest improvements in products and services; his employees are competent; and he is interested in our welfare because he understands that his interests are best served by meeting our needs fully.

5. *Accessibility:* He is conveniently located, so that he can furnish goods and services easily and promptly.

6. *Reputation:* He is reliable; he can fulfill his promises; and he is ethical in all his relationships with his customers, employees, and the community. He can provide evidence that he has furnished goods or services satisfactorily to other users whose requirements are similar to ours.

NEGOTIATING WITH SUPPLIERS

There are three principal methods by which the church selects its suppliers: "open-market buying," "competitive bidding," and "negotiated buying."

Open-Market Buying: This is the procedure we individuals use in personal and household purchasing. It is also widely used in church purchasing. "Open-Market Purchasing" means buying without negotiation. It consists of asking a selected vendor or group of vendors for price quotations on certain goods or services. Such inquiries are made to determine availability, the best delivery conditions, service facilities, and other factors affecting our purchasing decision. The vendor's reputation is an important factor in the buyer's judgment that the quoted price is a reasonable one. Implicit in open-market buying is the awareness of both parties that if at any time the buyer discovers that he is not being given the price and service arrangements he expects, he may obtain prices and place orders elsewhere. The vendor is still subject to competition, and very likely will give special attention to his "loyal" customers.

A drawback of the open-market buying method is that

the purchasing agent can be tempted to neglect the care and precision in the purchasing process that his church has the right to expect. When buying in the open market, the church's interest should be protected by: (1) frequently checking quoted prices against the last order price; (2) obtaining from vendors explanations of price increases; and (3) making frequent inquiries in the market to be sure that both the quality and price obtained is comparable to what the competition offers.

The National Association of Educational Buyer's handbook, *Purchasing for Educational Institutions,*[1] suggests the following circumstances in which the institutional buyer may place an order without negotation:

1. The purchasing official has previously negotiated a requirements contract to cover either a definite period of time or a definite dollar volume. In such cases, purchase orders are placed with the sources at the prices and under the conditions previously agreed upon.
2. The procurement official may have negotiated with the source of supply to buy all requirements of items that the supplier can furnish for an indefinite period of time, as needed. Such negotiations usually involve orders of fairly good size and cover a range of items. An example would be a buying arrangement worked out with a wholesale supplier of office supplies that are bought in standard package quantities for an office supply storeroom.
3. When the amount of a purchase is so small that negotiation time could not be justified, a petty cash purchase may be made or a purchase order may be issued without negotiation. There are, of course, many such small purchases to be made in every institution.

[1] James J. Ritterskamp, Jr., Forest L. Abbott, and Bert C. Ahrens, *Purchasing for Educational Institutions* (New York: Bureau of Publications, Teachers College, Columbia University, 1961), p. 63.

4. Some items can be obtained only from one source of supply. If the amount of a purchase is small, an unpriced purchase order may be the easiest way to handle it. If the cost is appreciable, negotiations certainly should be conducted as to price, delivery time, service required, and other factors.

5. Procurement officials may order on the basis of catalog information. The orders usually show either catalog prices or catalog prices less a known or negotiated institutional discount.

6. Orders may be placed without negotiation for other reasons. Sometimes a need is so urgent that a purchase order is issued immediately, the procurement official trusting a responsible supplier as to how the order will be priced and handled.

Competitive Bidding: Competitive bidding may be "formal" or "informal," but it always involves competition among prospective suppliers to provide specific merchandise or service. Let us look at the ways in which both formal bidding and informal bidding can be helpful to the church purchasing agent.

1. *Formal Competitive Bids:* Of all the methods of obtaining the best price for an established quality of merchandise or service, the formal competitive bid is the most precise and accurate. Typically, a formal bid proposal or "request for quotation" is either distributed officially to selected vendors or an advertisement in the public press invites any and all qualified vendors to submit a proposal on or before a certain date. Bids are opened at the appointed time, often at a public bid opening session, and the contract is awarded to the lowest bidder whose proposal conforms to all of the specifications.

The specifications must be established clearly in advance and the vendor must be given ample time to review them and to compute his price.

It is both an advantage and a weakness of formal bidding that it severely limits individual discretion and is relatively inflexible. Because of this and the considerable amount of time and effort required for its completion, a church should reserve formal bidding for:

a. Major capital improvements
b. Large-volume supplies
c. High-cost equipment
d. All inclusive package insurance contracts (see p. 155)

Since the formal bid will be used by the church mainly for large value purchases, the selection of the vendors who will be invited to bid becomes a matter of great sensitivity. Judgment has to be made carefully as to whether all available suppliers of a given item, or only a screened group, will be invited to submit bids. Here the matter of "home preference," discussed on pp. 165-166 is germane.

When inviting formal bids, most churches will find that a standard commercial "request for quotation" form, shown as Figure 4, will expedite the procedure, provide uniformity, and permit receiving quotations on identical specifications. By an ingenious use of spot-carbon, each of the suppliers receives an identical request that shows only his name and excludes the names of all other vendors.

After the formal bids have been received, the church purchasing official must review each submission to be sure that it conforms to all specifications of quality, quantity, delivery, and price. At times, samples will be submitted and these will have to be examined and tested.

A standard purchase order to the successful bidder officially completes the formal bidding transaction; however,

CROMWELL PRINTERY, INC   ALBANY 1, N. Y.

WASHINGTON HEBREW CONGREGATION

REQUEST FOR QUOTATION

Feruary 10, 1964

	VENDOR	QUOTATION	DELIVERY	F.O.B.	TERMS
1.	A B C Roofing Co. 9652 - 10th St. N.E. Washington, D. C. 20081	$ 6 per ft. $ 792 Total	by 4/1/64	—	net
2.	Midland Roofers, Inc. 2111 Fairway Avenue, S.E. Washington, D.C. 20029	$ 6.30 per ft. $ 831.60 Total	by 4/1/64	—	net
3.	Senior Contractors, Inc. 1829 Loring Street, N. W. Washington, D.C. 20084	$ 6.10 per ft. 805.20 Total less 16.10 disc. $ 789.10 net	by 4/1/64	—	2% cash 10 days
4.					
5.					

ADDRESS REPLY TO: WASHINGTON HEBREW CONGREGATION
 3935 MACOMB ST., N. W.
 WASHINGTON 16, D. C.

QUANTITY	DESCRIPTION
One Installation	Install expansion joint as required across the main Sanctuary roof, following the line of the existing patch and going the complete length of the roof - 132 ft. The expansion joint is to be installed in a workmanlike manner in conformance with the construction details as illustrated in Dow Chemical Company pamphlet AIA File #12-H, January 19, 1964, for the installation of an Ethafoam expansion strip.

BID TO CLOSE	TERMS & F.O.B. POINT	DELIVERY TIME REQUIRED
Feb. 26, '64	Specify cash or church discounts allowed	Order to be placed by 3/5/64 Job to be completed by 4/1/64

Figure 4. This preprinted "Request For Quotation" form permits inquiries to be made of up to five suppliers or contractors on a single typing. By an ingenious use of spot carbon each of the suppliers sees only his name and address in the heading but all receive identical descriptions of the merchandise or service desired. The requests may be mailed in a regular envelope. (Courtesy Washington Hebrew Congregation, Washington, D.C.)

common courtesy and sound business practice require that all unsuccessful bidders who were not present at the bid opening be notified, by letter or by telephone, that the negotiation for this item has been completed.

2. *Informal Bidding:* This has many of the advantages of the formal competitive bid and avoids some of its drawbacks.

When using the informal bid, the buyer usually will have preselected his suppliers and will solicit inquiries from a smaller list than would be used in formal bidding. The bids generally will be obtained by telephone, or by personal negotiation with salesmen, or by visits to suppliers. The telephone is the most convenient and frequently-used device for obtaining informal quotations.

Typically, the buyer will furnish a written list of items or describe what is wanted to one or more suppliers over the telephone. The vendors will then check their stocks and informally give the buyer the price, terms of delivery, and other aspects of the proposed transaction. When a satisfactory arrangement is made, purchase orders may be issued informally; but in all cases they should be confirmed by a written purchase order and the vendor's representative should be notified that such a confirmation is in the mail. If possible, the written purchase order should be executed while the arrangement is being made, or immediately thereafter, and the vendor should be informed of the serial number of the purchase order he will receive so that this number may appear on the invoice.

Use of the informal quotation saves considerable time and avoids a great deal, though not all, of the paperwork involved in formal bidding. However, it is important to remember that the object of bid quotations, whether formal or informal, is to create a framework within which a seller's offer to furnish an item or a service at a specified price can be converted into placement of an order. Therefore, the church buyer must be sure that even in an informal negotiation all the specifications and other terms of the contract are made as clear and precise as they would be if there were a formal bid.

When purchasing with competitive bidding—whether formal or informal—the church must follow two inviolable rules:

1. Do not request a supplier to bid if we know in advance that an order will not be issued to that supplier, even if his price should happen to be the lowest.
2. When several suppliers have been requested to furnish quotations, and there has been no deviation from the standard conditions and criteria that apply equally to all bidders, the award of the contract to the low bidder should be automatic and unquestioned.

These rules do not preclude rejection of a low bid. Sometimes there are valid reasons for such disqualifications. Evidence of unethical practices by a bidder, or of deliberate collusion between two or more suppliers, is sufficient reason for disqualifying a bidder. The bidder may be in such precarious financial condition as to cast doubt on his ability to fulfill the contract.

Still other situations will raise ethical questions in the church buyer's mind as to whether he should accept a bid. For instance, if a bid comes in much lower than was anticipated, and much lower than any of the competing bids, the buyer would have legal right to accept the low bid without question, award the contract, and then require compliance by the bidder. On the other hand, if the church has reason to believe that the supplier has, in good faith, made a serious error in computation, the purchasing agent is faced with a question: Does his duty to the church require that he insist on compliance with a price that will obviously cause a substantial loss to the supplier, or does he have an ethical obligation to the supplier to point out the error and give him an opportunity to refigure?

Cost-plus buying is justified only where costs cannot be determined with assurance in advance. Under this procedure the vendor or contractor, presumably one who has done work for the church previously and who has a reputation for honesty and accuracy, agrees to supply certain items or perform certain work for a price that is equal to the cost of "time and material," plus an agreed-upon profit.

In church purchasing this type of buying is used almost exclusively for large and complicated repair jobs where it is obviously difficult for the contractor to determine in advance the extent of the damage or to anticipate what impediments he may encounter. In the absence of such an arrangement the contractor might feel that in order to determine a fixed price that will protect him adequately, he would have to quote the maximum possible cost of the repair. Where the contractor is a reliable individual with a good reputation, the church purchasing agent may be justified in arranging for a cost-plus contract as an alternative. Usually, however, he is wise to insert an "upset" or "ceiling" price into the agreement, which would cover the maximum cost under any circumstances. These arrangements should be entered into reluctantly and with the knowledge that their use will require detailed supervision and verification.

When a vendor has been chosen carefully by any of the foregoing methods, the buyer will frequently find that an unsuccessful vendor will come in after negotiations are concluded and offer a lower price. This is "price chiseling" and it is a handicap to the church business manager who is trying to maintain an orderly and dignified operation.

We must insist at all times that a vendor's first price be his best price. When prices have been established through open-market purchasing or through informal or formal bidding, vendors should not be allowed to change their quotations to gain an unfair competitive advantage.

Another frustration to which the church purchasing agent is subject is the perennial "Monday morning quarterback" in the congregation. Without being fully aware of the specifications, requirements, or market conditions, this individual will often boast that he "could have bought it cheaper." Occasionally, of course, the critic may indeed known of a more desirable source, and, if so, the information should be filed for future reference. But when the church purchasing agent knows in his own mind that he has made a careful and thorough search of the market and that he has acquired the best value for his church, he must be sufficiently thick-skinned to withstand any chiseling of other suppliers and any carping of church members.

PLACING THE ORDER

Every purchase for the church account should be made with, or confirmed by, a written purchase authorization. Too often, order placement is a haphazard affair that leaves the church unprotected and frequently results in misunderstandings with the vendors.

A wide variety of pre-printed or stock purchase orders is available from commercial stationers, office supply houses, and specialized forms manufacturers.

Three purchase order forms suitable for use by churches of various sizes are shown as Figures 5, 6, and 7.

> *Figure 5.* Purchase order forms such as this one can be acquired from numerous forms manufacturers and are purchased directly from the manufacturers' representatives rather than from a commercial stationer. This form is used in a lightweight pin-feed portable register. It is prepared in triplicate; the original goes to the vendor, one carbon to the bookkeeper for inclusion in the purchase file and the third copy for audit and inventory purposes. (Courtesy Washington Hebrew Congregation, Washington, D.C.)

AUDIT COPY

BOOKKEEPER'S COPY

VENDOR'S COPY

PHONE: EM 2-7100

WASHINGTON HEBREW CONGREGATION
MASSACHUSETTS AVE. at MACOMB ST., N. W.
WASHINGTON 16, D. C.

PURCHASE ORDER

REQN. NO.	FOR	DATE REQUIRED	DATE
114	Budget Acct-905	5/21/63	5/3/63

TO:

General Duplicator Co.

437 51 st., N.W.

Washington, D.C.

SHIP TO → Washington Hebrew Congregation

Address as above

SHIP VIA: your truck   TERMS: net cash 30 days

QUANTITY	PLEASE ENTER OUR ORDER FOR THE FOLLOWING:	UNIT PRICE	
1	Ajax Stencil Duplicator –		
	Elec. Model 705 – 705.00		
	10% church discount 70.50	635	50
1	Electro-spray unit for above	170	00
1	Cabinet for above	45	00
1	Slip Sheeter	69	00
1	Extra Color Drum	29	00
	TOTAL	948	50
	TRADE-IN ALLOWANCE	100	00
	NET TOTAL	848	50

SHOW THIS NUMBER ON
ALL PACKAGES, INVOICES
AND REFERENCES TO THIS
PURCHASE ORDER NO.

1168

Julian Feldman

AUTHORIZED SIGNATURE

5-51-55-5 · PRINTED BY THE STANDARD REGISTER CO., DAYTON 1, OHIO, U. S. A.

First Congregational Church   PURCHASE ORDER

535 South Hoover Street
Los Angeles 5, California

PURCHASING OFFICE

N° 8632

Send All Bills to Purchasing Office   Date October 1, 1964

TO: Widget Hardware Emporium   Department No. 6
3935 Fulton Street
Los Angeles, California

QUANTITY		UNIT PRICE	NET AMOUNT
2	A-1 Rotary Lawnmowers - Model 65	$54.80	$109.60

By *Alva Baker* Business Manager
AUTHORIZED SIGNATURE

Figure 6. The larger church can consider printing its own, specially-tailored purchase order forms, like this one which is prepared in three-part pads, with hand-inserted carbon. (Courtesy First Congregational Church of Los Angeles.)

For the church, three copies are desirable. The original will go to the vendor; the second copy becomes a part of the purchase file that goes to the bookkeeper for ultimate payment; the third copy is kept in a numerical or chronological file for audit and other reference purposes.

Purchase orders usually should contain the following information:

1. A pre-printed heading, showing the name and address of the church.
2. Date of the order.
3. Terms of payment, including any cash discounts.
4. Name and address of the vendor.
5. Budget allocation against which the item will be charged.

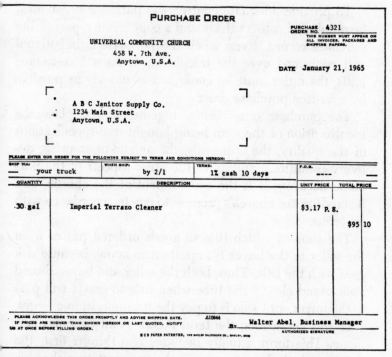

PURCHASE ORDER

PURCHASE ORDER NO. **4321**
THIS NUMBER MUST APPEAR ON ALL INVOICES, PACKAGES AND SHIPPING PAPERS.

UNIVERSAL COMMUNITY CHURCH
458 W. 7th Ave.
Anytown, U.S.A.

DATE **January 21, 1965**

A B C Janitor Supply Co.
1234 Main Street
Anytown, U.S.A.

PLEASE ENTER OUR ORDER FOR THE FOLLOWING SUBJECT TO TERMS AND CONDITIONS HEREON:

SHIP VIA: your truck	WHEN SHIP: by 2/1	TERMS: 1% cash 10 days	F.O.B. ----

QUANTITY	DESCRIPTION	UNIT PRICE	TOTAL PRICE
30 gal	Imperial Terrazo Cleaner	$3.17 P. G.	
			$95 10

PLEASE ACKNOWLEDGE THIS ORDER PROMPTLY AND ADVISE SHIPPING DATE. IF PRICES ARE HIGHER THAN SHOWN HEREON OR LAST QUOTED, NOTIFY US AT ONCE BEFORE FILLING ORDER.

Δ10844

By **Walter Abel, Business Manager**
AUTHORIZED SIGNATURE

NCR PAPER PATENTED, THE SHELBY SALESBOOK CO., SHELBY, OHIO

Figure 7. Purchase order forms like this one can be pre-printed in two, three or four part sets or purchased in pads from a commercial stationery house. If purchased in blank, the name of the church can be imprinted in the church office from an addressograph plate. (Courtesy Shelby Salesbook Co., Shelby, Ohio.)

6. Any special contract terms.
7. Shipping or delivery instructions, including any essential information about wrapping, carrier, and specific delivery point.
8. Quantity.
9. Full description of the item.
10. Unit price.
11. Price extension for the total quantity.
12. Signature of the authorized purchasing agent, with his title.
13. The number of the order (either at the top or bottom margin).

To provide adequate control, the purchase order must be numbered consecutively and a copy made a part of the purchase record. Even when the purchase is negotiated and confirmed over the telephone, or on a face-to-face basis, the order must be confirmed as quickly as possible by a written purchase order.

The purchase order brings together in one place the identification of the item being bought, the specifications of the quality, the approvals, the agreed-upon-price, delivery conditions, and all of the other aspects of the purchase decision. It is the commitment of the church, and it stands as the church's promise to pay in accordance with its terms.

The time at which title to goods ordered passes from the seller to the buyer is important to know, because risk goes with the title. Thus, both the seller and buyer should understand clearly the time when title to goods will pass to the buyer, and who is to pay the transportation charges.

In this connection the term F.O.B. Point becomes germane. This term actually includes two things: first, the point to which the shipper pays the transportation charges; and second, the determination, from a legal standpoint, of the time at which title passes to the buyer. There are several methods of paying the transportation charges. The following are the most commonly used:

"F.O.B. Shipping Point." The shipper assumes the responsibility for the goods until they reach the railroad, truck depot, or express office. At this point, the title passes to the buyer and he pays the rest of the charges.

"F.O.B. City of Destination." The shipper pays all the transportation charges to the city in which the buyer is located. The buyer pays the cartage charges from the freight station to his own place of business. The title passes to the buyer when the goods arrive at the city of destination.

"F.O.B. the Buyer's Place of Business." The shipper pays all transportation charges. The title passes when the shipment arrives at the buyer's place of business.

Petty Cash Purchases: It is sometimes advantageous to make small purchases out-of-pocket, by-passing the normal purchasing procedure. Provided this practice is kept within bounds, it can reduce the amount of red tape and result in much convenience and saving to the church. However, limits should be placed on the kinds of cash purchases that can be made—a dollar limit as well as a limit on the type of material that can be bought through the petty cash account. Without such limits, there is possibility of abuse.

Petty cash purchases can be handled in two ways. One is to advance cash to the purchaser prior to the actual purchase. Thus, a teacher in the church school can be advanced cash for the purchase of certain play-time materials she wishes to choose from the shelf selection of a nearby store. In this case, of course, the teacher would be required to submit a petty cash voucher, together with a cash register receipt or sales slip for post-audit verification. Under another method, she could make the purchase out-of-pocket with her own funds and submit her petty cash voucher for reimbursement.

As we have pointed out, the use of a cash basis for purchasing some items below a fixed dollar amount has some advantages in terms of savings in clerical costs. However, the possibility of abuse is so great, particularly where several persons are purchasing for the church account, that its use should be strictly limited and controlled.

C.O.D. and Pre-paid Purchases: These should also be

discouraged whenever possible since they are expensive, time-consuming, and often can lead to confusion. For one thing, it is impossible to make an inspection of the contents of the C.O.D. purchase before the item is paid for. This increases the difficulty of making adjustments and filing claims. There are, however, occasional situations where C.O.D. or pre-paid purchases can work to the advantage of the church. These occur where a special discount is offered for advance payment or C.O.D. payment. At other times, it would be essential to pre-pay purchases; for example, for Government-printed, stamped envelopes.

Another example of purchases that are often made on a pre-paid basis is that of subscriptions to publications. It is common practice to reduce the per-copy rate sharply as the length of the subscription period increases. Publishers sometimes offer additional advantages in terms of discount or additional length of subscription if it is paid in advance.

Finally, there are occasions when a large order will be given to a vendor who is unable to finance the complete cost of the contracted item over a long period of time, without at least partial payments from the purchaser. Thus, it is not uncommon for a church or any other builder to pay a general contractor in installments during the course of construction. It is common also for a church to make a deposit payment in advance when a contract is signed for the construction of a new organ. Such a contract generally calls for additional payments to be made to the contractor at the time the installment begins and during the course of the installation, with the final payment being deferred until the installation has been completed and checked.

Emergency and Rush Orders: No matter how effective

a system is established, there will be times when an order must be handled on a "rush" or "emergency" basis.

Emergency purchases usually mean greater expense. It is more difficult to make a careful selection of vendors and to take the necessary time to seek out all the quotations we might wish to receive. It is not only the church purchasing agent who is disturbed. Vendors are usually displeased with a rush procedure and this will often result in higher prices. However, since rush and emergency purchases *will* occur, it is important that procedures be flexible enough to assure that the accounting office will maintain uniform records and that appropriate authorizations are received at all levels.

All too often, the so-called "rush" order results from faulty inventory control, poor planning or budgeting, a lack of confidence in the church purchasing agent by certain using departments, or from sheer bad habit. But there are valid emergencies, also. Sometimes such emergency situations result from a breakdown or failure of equipment or from a new program need that arises suddenly and that must be met immediately. Even the most highly organized system should be flexible enough to provide for the orderly handling of such exceptional situations.

With the signing of the purchase order, the church buyer can give a sigh of relief and push his chair back from his desk. He has completed the basic part of the purchasing process. The need for the goods or services has been determined and expressed. He has decided on the right quantity and the right time of delivery. He has put together the right combination of quality and price to acquire the maximum possible value. And he has successfully negotiated with the vendor and chosen the most appropriate one to supply his church. But he is not yet finished. All he has done up to this point can be negated and wasted if appropriate follow-up is not given to the order.

Chapter 8

AFTER THE PURCHASE
ORDER IS PLACED

No PURCHASE is complete until the goods have been received by the church, accepted, delivered to the user, or placed into storage and a bill for the item presented for payment. On page 21, we listed 17 elements of the purchasing process. Eight of these—almost half of the total—occur after the purchase order is placed. In this chapter, we will examine some of these elements.

ACCEPTANCE OF THE ORDER

A purchase agreement, like any other contract, requires the consent of both parties. If our purchase order has been placed following the receipt of a written quotation, then we do have such mutual consent, provided we have accepted the vendor's offer exactly as he presented it. Otherwise, we can never be quite sure that our order will be acted on until we receive a written acceptance from the vendor.

It is important legally that acceptance be in exact terms of the offer. If, in his acceptance, the church buyer has changed the nature of the offer, this constitutes a new offer rather than the closing of the contract. For example, if a stationery supply firm offers the church a substantial quantity of mimeograph paper at a certain price, and the purchasing agent agrees to purchase this amount of paper but at a different price, then this is not a contract. The new price offered by the purchasing agent is a counter-offer.

In general, an offer remains in effect until it expires, is revoked, is rejected, or is accepted. A supplier often will set a time limit within which his offer must be accepted, such as, "This offer must be accepted within 60 days."

If the offer is not accepted within the stated period, it is no longer in effect. The person making an offer may also revoke it any time prior to its acceptance.

Most vendors with whom the church purchasing agent deals do not acknowledge purchase orders sent to them unless requested to do so. For most items bought by the church, it is not important that a formal acceptance of the purchase order be received. Generally, delivery of the goods will constitute the appropriate acceptance. However, there are some instances where it is important that the church office know immediately after the order has been placed that it has been accepted by the vendor, subject to all the conditions that have been written into the purchase order. In such cases, it is desirable to type a special written request, attach it to the purchase order, asking that a formal acknowledgment be returned.

CHANGES AND CANCELLATIONS

No matter how careful we have been throughout the purchasing procedure, from the original statement of need to completion of the purchase order, situations will occur where, for good and substantial reasons, we will wish to change the order. Perhaps a requisition for certain maintenance supplies at the parsonage will be received shortly after a purchase order for similar supplies at the main church building has been entered. A change order to increase the quantity might also be called for in order to take advantage of any quantity discount that might be forthcoming. Similarly, we may wish to change the time or place of delivery, or perhaps simply to correct a clerical mistake made when writing the order.

For most church situations, neither the volume of purchase orders nor the number of potential changes are sufficient to warrant maintaining supplies of a specialized change form. One convenient way of handling a change is simply to write it on a new purchase order, noting in large letters that this is a change order and referring to the original purchase order number and date. Another satisfactory way—perhaps the most usual way of handling a change—is by ordinary correspondence: a letter from the church purchasing agent to the vendor. Whether the change order is made by special form or by letter, the vendor should be given complete information on the item to be changed and the modification desired. Thus, in our example cited above, a letter change might be handled as follows:

UNIVERSAL COMMUNITY CHURCH
458 West 7th Avenue
Anytown, U.S.A.

ABC Janitor Supply Company
4519 Traymore Street
Anytown, U.S.A.

Attention: Mr. Sellers

Sir:

Please make the following change on our purchase order number 4321, dated January 21, 1965, as follows:

From: One 30-gallon drum Imperial Terrazzo Cleaner
at $3.17 per gallon.

To: Two 30-gallon drums Imperial Terrazzo Cleaner
at $3.02 per gallon.

Additional delivery instructions

Please deliver one 30-gallon drum to our main building
at the address shown on our letterhead above. The other
drum is to be delivered to our church parsonage at 9876
Tranquility Drive.

Please sign the carbon copy of this letter and return it to
us.

Your cooperation will be very much appreciated.

Sincerely yours,

Walter Abel
Business Manager

Change noted: ABC CO.
Date _____

Note that this letter provides for acceptances of the
change order by the vendor. This is desirable because a
change order is, in effect, a new purchase order, and all the
requirements for acceptance apply here just as to the original purchase order. It is important also that copies of the
change order be attached to each copy of the purchase order remaining in the church office, including the bookkeeping and audit copies.

A cancellation is a specialized kind of change order.
Cancellations may be called for: (1) because the vendor
has failed to deliver the merchandise on time; or (2) because changed conditions have eliminated or modified the
need for the merchandise.

In the former instance, the church might even have a legal claim to recover any monetary losses suffered because of failure to receive the material on time. Such losses will generally be very difficult to prove and even more difficult to collect on. However, for large contracts, particularly in connection with major construction, reimbursement for such losses is possible and desirable.

In the more usual situation, an order is cancelled because the church itself no longer needs or desires the materials. In this case, the church may be liable for costs incurred by the vendor, assuming the vendor had been willing and able to fulfill his responsibilities under the contract and had made a formal acceptance of the order.

In the normal course of events, when comfortable, ongoing relationships have been established with vendors, and the goods in question are nonperishable shelf items, no question of reimbursement arises. However, if the vendor has gone to considerable expense in preparing to deliver a cancelled order the church may be charged full or partial cost. Mimeograph paper cut to special sizes, or ordered in special colors not normally stocked by the church's distributor, would be one example. A printed brochure for which some type has already been set, art work drawn, and special paper cut to size, would be other examples of cancellations requiring that the church reimburse the vendor for his expenses.

Cancellations must always be in writing and issued in the same manner as a change order, either by letter or by special forms. Here again, the notification of cancellation should include the original purchase order number, and the item or items that are being eliminated should be clearly stated.

The changed conditions justifying cancellation of an order do *not* include the fact that the purchasing agent has discovered, after he has mailed the purchase order, that he can buy the item at a lower price from some other supplier. Such actions are considered "sharp practice." Just as the church buyer expects the vendor to perform his part of the purchase contract satisfactorily, despite any unexpected changes in the market price or supply situation, so the church is expected to fulfill its obligations, even if the market conditions should change to its advantage.

PENALTY CLAUSES

The church purchasing agent is always concerned that the terms of his purchase agreement be complied with by the vendor. The problem arises, however, as to how far he should go in writing in provisions for his legal protection, considering that he wants to maintain good vendor relations. We do not want to make it too difficult for the vendor to do business with us.

Some purchase order forms include a statement such as the following:

> Acceptance of this purchase order by the vendor guarantees that delivery will be made by the date stated hereon. In the event delivery is not made by the date stated above, we reserve the right to cancel the order and to charge the vendor the full cost of any loss incurred by reason of such nondelivery.

It is possible to go further and include penalty clauses calling for *liquidated damages* in the event of failure to deliver on time or in the proper quantity. It is usually unrealistic to do this. In most cases, such provisions are simply a pious hope, and in many instances their inclusion might cause the vendor to reject the order. Yet, reserving the right of cancellation, or of claiming damages, does not accomplish our basic purpose—of getting the merchandise we need in conducting the affairs of the church. Moreover, the determination of what is a reasonable time beyond which one should exercise his right of cancellation is very difficult. The determination of what actual loss or damage is suffered by the institution as a result of non-delivery is even more difficult. Who is to express a dollar value for the failure to receive promised choir robes in time for a special festival service?

Still, there are times when an order being placed is of such importance as to require some firm assurance that delivery will be made by the specified time. One way would be to insert a "liquidated damages" clause, which would state a definite delivery date or time, such as, "on or before 5 p.m., July 15, 1965." Ideally, a specific penalty should also be included in this liquidated damage clause. This may be either a lump sum or a per-diem amount, such as, "$15 per eight-hour working day, Monday through Friday." A performance bond underwritten by an insurance company is another device to insure compliance with the terms of a purchase agreement. This is usually limited to such areas as construction, and usually applies to the fulfillment of the whole contract rather than just for delivery of a specific item. Usually, the cost of this additional protection is justified only if actual expenses will be incurred if the delivery dates are not met, or if serious damage to the church program will result as a result of failure to perform as contracted.

ORDER FOLLOW-UP

Follow-up on an order can be a routine, normal operation, or it can be an unplanned, haphazard procedure, replete with emergency phone calls, frantic tracing, and missed deadlines. It is an important procedure but it need not be complicated. In most churches, a simple "tickler" file and a good memory are all that is required. In the larger churches, it may be desirable to have a more highly organized, automatic system of follow-up, with a written set of procedures and instructions, so that all orders having a firm delivery date are followed up and checked automatically.

Some orders will require no follow-up whatever. Others will demand frequent and systematic attention. Where a delivery date has been set on the purchase order in accordance with the demands of the using department, it is important that follow-up on an order be far enough in advance of the delivery date, to insure that any possible delays can be taken care of through alternative sources of supply. Follow-ups with vendors in the same city usually can be made over the telephone. For out-of-city suppliers, a letter with an enclosed self-addressed postcard may be desirable.

It is neither possible nor desirable to have an exact and precise follow-up procedure that will be exactly the same for each order. No two purchase orders are exactly alike. A great deal depends on who our vendor is, how well we know him, what our experience has been, the nature of the goods that have been ordered, the urgency attached to the delivery date, and the needs of the using department.

"RECEIVING" VS. "ACCEPTING"

It is possible for *any* employee to receive merchandise physically. Too often this is just what happens. The first person the delivery man meets, whether he is a part-time custodian or the pastor, signs for the delivery and tells the drayman to put the merchandise in some inconspicuous place. There it is likely to sit until it gets in somebody's way or the person who originally ordered it starts a frantic search around the building for it.

Such haphazard procedures are not suited to a well-organized church. There must be a central receiving station, and all delivery men should be immediately directed to that station by an easily visible sign or orally. A central receiving point can be a great time-saver for all personnel. By reducing the occasions when shipments will be lost, stolen, or mislaid, the efficiency of the entire procedure is increased and uniformity in handling deliveries is assured. Establishing one central receiving point in the church automatically fixes the responsibility for accepting and safeguarding shipments of merchandise. It will be appreciated by vendors—and their delivery men, too, since it conserves their time and energy.

A central receiving point is not necessarily the same thing as a central assembly point (where received merchandise is held temporarily), although it may be. At a central receiving point, a knowledgeable employee examines the invoice, determines the proper place for the merchandise to be placed, determines (to the extent possible, without opening the packages or cases) that the appropriate number of articles or containers as stated on the invoice has been received, and that there has been no visible damage in shipment.

In many churches, the central receiving point will be the church office—the one place in the building where knowledgeable personnel are almost sure to be found at any time of the normal working day. Larger churches frequently have a station at one of the back or side entrances of the building, where the head maintenance man has his desk and files, as well as facilities for receiving and checking in merchandise. Other churches are fortunate enough to have a doorkeeper or watchman at the main entrance to greet and direct visitors. This can serve as the central receiving station. If concealed space near the main entrance can be provided for a small receiving room, the person in charge can also serve as the principal receiving clerk.

There are many ways in which the receiving procedure can be implemented. The important thing is that there *be* a procedure and that it be followed. It is important for both legal and administrative reasons that there be rules, clearly understood by all employees, spelling out exactly how goods are to be received, signed for, protected, and stored. These rules should also state clearly the procedure for inspecting and making final acceptance of goods. They should also provide for seeing to it that the receiving ticket and any other supporting papers are delivered to the accounting department immediately, so that any cash discounts for which the church is eligible are taken. Finally, it is essential that the requisitioning department be notified immediately that the merchandise has arrived and is waiting.

It may be helpful to develop a check-list form that would be completed at the central receiving depot, attached to the delivery ticket, and forwarded to the office. Such a check-list might contain the following:

RECEIVING CHECK-LIST

I. (Each item to be initialed by person receiving goods)
1. Date and time of receipt: _____
2. Delivered by: (Name of carrier or company) ____
   _____
3. Date and time of delivery: _____
4. No. of cartons, bundles, cases, barrels, or other containers in shipment: _____
5. Any visible damage to merchandise or its container (Be sure this damage is noted on the carrier's delivery ticket): _____

_____

_____

II. (To be completed by inspector or using department)
  1. Requisition number: _____
  2. Concealed damage noted: _____
  3. Deviations from original order: _____
  4. Acceptance approved: _____
     Rejection recommended: _____

_____

_____

III. (To be completed by bookkeeper)
  1. Purchase order number: _____
  2. Requisition number: _____
  3. Cash discount provided: _____
  4. Approved for payment by check number: _____

Once the goods have been received and evidence of this receipt has been forwarded to the appropriate authorities, are we finished? Not quite. Any employee of the church can physically *receive* the goods, and once they have been received, the church and its employees have a responsibility for safeguarding them, protecting them from the weather, and keeping track of their physical presence. However, they are still not officially the church's property. There still remains the need to "inspect" the goods in order to verify that the item received is exactly what has been ordered. The goods must then be formally "accepted."

Inspection: As noted earlier, the person who first receives the merchandise should inspect the exterior condition of packages before signing the bill of lading or truck driver's ticket. If it appears that a package has been broken or otherwise damaged, this fact should be noted on the bill of lading or truck ticket. An unqualified receipt should not be given the delivery man unless the packages are, to all outward appearances, undamaged. If, at a later date, it is discovered that the contents of the package were damaged, it is still possible to file a claim against the transportation company. If concealed damage is later discovered, the carrier should be notified promptly and a claim filed. The carrier should be given an opportunity to inspect the goods.

After the containers have been opened a physical inspection should be made of the merchandise to make certain that the material received conforms in all respects to the specifications for what was ordered. Where necessary, the merchandise should be sampled and tested by the using department as quickly as possible, and a formal approval and acceptance indicated on the receiving ticket, as noted above.

If we discover some deficiency or error, we have the choice of rejecting the delivery outright and returning it to the vendor at his expense or accepting the goods even though they do not conform to the specifications. In such situations, it may be necessary for the vendor to restore the goods to the desired condition or to make a monetary or quantity allowance for any deficiency.

PAYING FOR MERCHANDISE

An invoice is notification of shipment. It puts the buyer on notice as to what has been shipped and the nature of the claim that has been established by the vendor against the church. It constitutes a definite claim against the church and therefore should be handled with care and under a definite procedure.

Most suppliers mail the invoice as soon as the goods have been cleared for shipment. Accordingly, the invoice will sometimes arrive at the church prior to actual delivery of the goods. Since time is of the essence in taking advantage of cash discounts for prompt payment, the matter of when the discount period begins is important. In the case of a 2 per cent cash discount for payment "within 10 days," does the 10-day period begin to run when the invoice is mailed, when the invoice is received, or when the merchandise is received? Many suppliers state on their invoice that their discount period begins with the day of mailing the invoice. Since the cash discount is a consideration extended by the vendor at his option, this severe limitation will have to govern, unless the purchase agreement has clearly stated otherwise in advance. However, in the absence of such a restriction by the vendor, most churches can assume that the discount period begins to run after the goods are received. One way of avoiding this problem is to include a standard clause on the purchase order, such as the following: "Unless otherwise noted on this purchase order, payment terms shall be considered to be 2 per cent, 10 days, with the discount period to commence after delivery of materials and receipt of invoice in proper form."

COMPLETING THE PURCHASE FILE

With receipt of the goods, inspection and acceptance, and approval of the invoice for payment, the purchase transaction is complete. The bookkeeper can then prepare the payment voucher and the unsigned check, which is forwarded to the appropriate disbursing office together with all the supporting documents for payment to the vendor. When the check has been signed and sent to the vendor, the voucher is attached and the purchase file is complete.

Chapter 9

INVENTORY, STORAGE, AND RECORDS

Two BASIC ELEMENTS of inventory control are essential for churches. One is that of maintaining an adequate supply for a specified period of time. We are still talking about quantity, just as we were in Chapter 4, but in inventory planning we are not so much concerned with actual numbers of items, pounds, barrels, or pieces. We are more concerned about the quantity we will need for a specific *period of use*. This period of use—the days, the weeks, the months, the years of supply quantity—becomes a controlling element not only in determining how much is to be purchased, but also in managing stocks. Determining the proper period of supply is most crucial, because stocks that are "too small," "too large," or "improperly balanced" ultimately impose purchasing and other administrative tasks that rob dollars from important church programs.

Lead-time is the second basic factor in inventory control. Lead-time is the period that elapses from the time we declare that an item is needed to the time the purchased item is delivered and ready for use. If our inventory plan is to provide adequate protection against the opposite extremes of "too little" and "too much," the right quantity must be ordered at the right time. Let us look at some of the ways we can achieve this kind of precision.

CENTRAL STORAGE FACILITIES

In most churches, storage facilities are maintained for at least eight separate classifications of items:

1. *Office Supplies and Small Equipment:* No matter how small the office, a cabinet or closet should be maintained for such items as stationery, typing paper, carbon paper, paper clips, staplers and staples, paper punches, and file binders. The way this basic storage facility is maintained in a church is one indication of the efficiency of its office management. Where these items are stored in neat, logical sequence, in an easily accessible location, and in a manner in which they are easily identifiable, the management of the church's office function is likely to be efficient, systematic, and careful. When the office supply storage facility is a helter-skelter jumble, one may wonder whether the business affairs of the church are handled in an effective manner.

2. *Duplicating and Mail Room Supplies:* Duplicating paper and envelopes should be stacked neatly on shelves immediately above and around the duplicating, addressing, and folding machinery. Paper supply shelves should permit re-stacking of unused portions of duplicating paper reams without wastage. Envelopes should be kept in their original boxes to avoid mixing different kinds and sizes, and a sample of the contents should be stapled to the front of the box to permit quick identification.

3. *School Supplies:* Construction paper, crayons, paste, blunt scissors, chalk, erasers, flannel board, flash cards, slide and motion picture projectors, screens and other visual-aid materials and equipment, textbooks, and the

myriad items used in an education program should be centrally stored and easily available to all authorized personnel.

4. *Sacramental and Ritual Objects:* The most reverential protection should be given to these items not only because of their sacred nature, but because they are frequently delicate, fragile, and extremely expensive to replace. Such objects should be stored securely in a well-ordered area, convenient to the sanctuary.

5. *Music:* A separate storage facility convenient to the choir-loft and easily accessible to the music minister, choir director, and organist should be maintained. Music is expensive and contributes greatly to the beauty and dignity of the liturgy. It is essential that music personnel be able to keep track of it in an orderly manner. Specially constructed racks can easily be made by any handyman. Special music filing boxes are available from commercial supply houses.

6. *Furniture:* Extra folding chairs that are needed only occasionally should be kept in concealed areas, preferably on mobile carts or on permanent storage racks. They should be stored in such a way as to protect them from needlessly scratching one another and still be quickly and easily available. The area under the stage in an auditorium or multipurpose room is especially convenient for storing surplus chairs and folding tables.

7. *Maintenance and Repair Supplies and Equipment:* Cleaning supplies, furnace filters, mop buckets, buffers, electric light bulbs, fluorescent starters, and related items should be stored in a well-ventilated, convenient location. Most modern church buildings provide several tiled and ventilated sink closets in various areas around the building, at least one on each level, to make it convenient for

maintenance personnel to keep cleaning supplies neat, orderly, and sweet-smelling. Larger churches should have, in addition, a central storehouse in a basement area where cleaning and maintenance supplies are kept in quantity and are easily available for future use. Frequently, it is possible to create such a protective area by erecting a simple frame in a corner of the basement and closing it off with wire netting.

8. *Landscape and Garden Supplies and Equipment:* Though these items in the small church can often be successfully stored with other maintenance and repair supplies and equipment, materials for landscape work such as fertilizers, pesticides, herbicides, ice melting compounds, and other chemicals are best stored in protected, elevated, ventilated, and dry areas in such a way that they will not contaminate one another. Preferably, there should be a minimum grade ramp directly to the outside, so that one man can easily move tractors, lawn mowers, and other heavy items.

Churches are not in the warehousing business, of course, but they do have an obligation to maintain an adequate inventory and to achieve optimum savings from quantity discounts consistent with the most efficient use of storage facilities. The basic purpose of a storage system is to receive and distribute, in the most efficient and economical manner, the goods required by all phases of the congregational program. The way storage is carried out is extremely important to the success of purchasing. This is as true for the simple installation of a few shelves in the church office as for the separate storehouse facilities required by some of the large churches. Careful planning when designing new buildings or remodeling old ones can contribute greatly to the success of the storage operation. But even in antiquated buildings, an imaginative search of the back corners in the interstices of the structure often yield surprising results in uncovering easily adaptable storage space that is presently going to waste.

Special attention should be given to waxes, solvents, oil, and other flammables. Safety experts recommend that such materials be located in a separate storeroom, preferably surrounded by fire walls and with a steel access door. Ideally, they should be in a shed or other building physically separate from the main buildings of the church. Although most janitor supply houses furnish liquid wax and solvents in drums that must be stored on a horizontal cradle in order for the spigot to operate properly, many insurance underwriters recommend that such drums be kept vertical and the contents removed by pumping.

Inventory items should be disbursed in rotation so as to minimize their deterioration. In commercial merchandising, this rotation is called FIFO (First In, First Out). This means, simply, that the older stock is always moved to such a position that it, rather than the new stock, will be drawn first. The little extra time and trouble taken in storing the materials in this way can avoid much deterioration and waste.

In a large church, which has several departments headquartered in various parts of the church building, or even in separate buildings, the temptation is often strong for each department to maintain a separate office supply facility. This is not to say that a secretary may never have an extra roll of transparent tape in her desk, but it is patently wasteful of both space and money to maintain completely separate and fully stocked cabinets of office supplies in the business office, the pastor's office, the education office, and the music library. A central supply room or cabinet should be under the control of one individual, and all departments and personnel of the church should draw from it.

INVENTORY RECORDS

It is essential that accurate records of stocks be maintained, but they need not be involved or cumbersome. There are two basic types of inventory control:

1. *The Perpetual Inventory:* This is a continuous record of stock receipts and disbursements, with a balance automatically calculated each time an entry is made.
2. *The Periodic Physical Inventory:* This is a tedious and time-consuming chore, which most churches do not find desirable or practical to perform more than once every year or two. The periodic, piece-by-piece, inventory usually is on a schedule determined by the auditors or by the insurance underwriter. For insurance purposes, the periodic inventory, particularly of major equipment, should be taken at least every three years in order to make certain that the insurance protection is for an adequate current replacement value. A type of perpetual inventory record that is convenient to use in virtually all aspects of the church's supply system is a visible card record, maintained within or immediately adjacent to the storage facility.

The purpose of maintaining inventory records is to help assure that an adequate supply of all materials and supplies is available when needed. To accomplish this, we must have a relatively automatic procedure for insuring that the inventory of any item stocked is replenished before the supply is exhausted.

The simplest form of automatic re-order reminder is the "last-box" system. This means that the moment we open the last box of carbon paper, the last case of paper towels, the last box of staples, or the last carton of sacramental candles the user automatically requisitions a new supply of this item.

Often this informal system is sufficient. However, it is too haphazard to be satisfactory in all situations. For one thing, the period of use of a single container will vary tremendously from commodity to commodity. For example, a single carton of sacramental candles may provide a 2-month supply, whereas the last box of 500 No. 10 envelopes may provide only a 30-minute supply during a mailing. If it takes two weeks from the time the order is placed with a printer until new envelopes are delivered, we will have an inconvenient stock-out during the intervening period. The simplest way is to place a red mark to "flag" the supply point on the stock record card, so that when a disbursement is posted that cuts the balance below this point, a requisition is automatically entered.

Generally speaking, we will start our replenishment requisition at a minimum of two lead-time periods before our zero point. This rule of thumb, of course, can be adjusted to a limited degree in order to expand the minimum lead-time amount into the quantity that will give us the most favorable price break.

A relatively simple reminder system for forms and stationery is that of placing a distinctively colored sheet of paper at the "minimum supply" point in the forms bin or on the forms shelf. Whenever the stock diminishes to this point, the colored re-order blank tells us that it is time to replace supplies.

The inventory records referred to in this chapter are the minimum that even the simplest purchasing procedure should include. Following are some other purchasing records many churches will find useful:

Equipment and Property File: A card record of all

equipment is extremely valuable. This includes a listing
of the type of equipment, the serial and model numbers,
the date purchased, the initial cost, the servicing record,
and the disposal record. (See Fig. 8.) This kind of file provides not only some valuable information for servicing or
replacing equipment, but also a needed record for insurance and audit control purposes.

Supplier File: Many church purchasing agents will find
useful an alphabetical listing of names, addresses, and telephone numbers of all regular suppliers, together with the
salesmen's names. When maintained either in a loose-leaf

WASHINGTON HEBREW CONGREGATION

Class or Type of Equipment __Stencil Duplicator, Electric__　　　Property Tag No.__411__

P R O P E R T Y   R E C O R D   C A R D

Description __Ajax Elec. Stencil Duplicator,__
with cabinet, sprayer, slip shtr.

		Repairs and Maintenance		
	Date	Description	By	Amount
Catalog or Model No. __705__	5/15/63	Instructions	Genl. Sup.	$ N.C.
MFG's Serial No. __53263__	7/10/63	Adjustments	" "	$ N.C.
Purchased from Genl. Duplicator Co.	9/20/63	"	" "	$ N.C
	11/4/63	Paper Jammed	" "	$ N.C
Date Purchased __May 3, 1963__	1/8/64	Order Adjust.	" "	$ N.C.
Invoice Amount __$ 947 50__	3/16/64	Broken Ink Knob	" "	$ N.C.
Shipping Expense __$ —__	4/20/64	Contract Call	" "	$ N.C.
Taxes __$ —__	6/18/64	Contract (Replaced		$
Installation Charge __$ —__		bent paper grip)	" "	$ 3.85
Total Cost __$ 947 50__				$
Trade-in Allowance __$ 100 00__				$
Net Cash Paid __$ 847 50__				$
Service Contract* __$ 42 00__				$

* 4/20/64 - One call bi-monthly for one year; 1st call 4/64, last call 2/64. Automatically renewed each year except on one month's prior notice by either party. Parts
extra.

Figure 8. Property control cards such as this can be prepared in the church office to provide a complete and convenient record of office equipment from purchase to disposal.
Additional service records and disposal records appear on
the reverse side. Corresponding property tag numbers can be
placed on the equipment for easy identification during audit
or inventory. (Courtesy Washington Hebrew Congregation,
Washington, D.C.)

book or a wheel index file, this is a convenient record for rapidly determining sources of supply. This record can provide a readily available list of vendors from whom prices will be solicited. It can include both the approved list of tried-and-tested firms with whom the church has dealt, as well as new firms that are to be invited to submit bids when opportunities arise.

Numerical Purchase Order File: This easily mantained record is an invaluable check source in the event the completed purchase file is ever mislaid or unavailable. It is also useful to the church auditor, or to a property appraiser for insurance purposes.

The important thing to remember in any purchase record system is that these records are desirable only if they provide needed information to augment experience, *and only if they are used.* Records of purchase and supply transactions should be geared to help the buyer explain and justify actions. However, the maintenance of a wide variety of statistical data and records, merely because "somebody thinks it is a good idea," is a waste of time and effort.

Once again, the guideline is, "keep it simple."

SURPLUS DISPOSAL AND SCRAP

If purchasing has been done in an intelligent and systematic manner, the problems the church will face in surplus disposal will be minimal. With conservative buying and careful evaluation of needs, the church will not accumulate valuable quantities of unusable materials. Occasionally, however, some items must be disposed of. Perhaps a few pieces of furniture still are usable after the lounge has been refurbished; or the maintenance department has graduated to a small tractor with a snow plow attachment, making surplus a walking snow-blower and mowing machine; or the introduction of a new bookkeeping machine has made surplus a stock of old forms.

Some items will suggest their own methods of disposal. Obsolete stationery, together with surplus or obsolete forms, can be gathered together periodically and sent to a local printer or binder for cutting and padding into convenient memoranda and scratch-pads. Equipment that is rendered obsolete because of the introduction of more modern machinery can be sold on the open market or used as a trade-in.

Another disposal problem occurs with *re-usable containers*. The most obvious of these, of course, is the soft-drink bottle that has a deposit value. These are rarely overlooked. However, other re-usable containers are used by the church. Cleaning materials and solvents frequently come in drums; these have a value either in cash or as credit. Many churches have a battery-operated emergency lighting system; distilled water for these comes in re-usable jugs that have a cash return value. A regular procedure for cashing in these containers will help keep the premises clear of unsightly "junk," and, over a period of a year, will result in measurable cash revenue or savings. At the same time, we must be economical in preparing material for disposal. It is obviously unwise to spend $25 on classified advertising for disposal of a piece of obsolete machinery that will bring only approximately $25. In this, as in so many aspects of the purchasing process, common sense will dictate the answer.

The cardinal rule to observe in the disposal of excess or obsolete items is that *no person has the right to give away or sell at less than the market value any item belonging to*

the church. Property, even surplus property, is an asset of
the church. It is worth money. Failure to safeguard its
value is every bit as wrong as diverting cash revenues of
the church to private purposes.

Chapter 10

BUYING EQUIPMENT: SOME SPECIAL CONSIDERATIONS

WHY EQUIPMENT IS SPECIAL

MOST CHURCHES own a considerable amount of a wide variety of equipment. Almost any church office may have at least one typewritter, one adding machine, and one duplicating machine. And, as the church grows in size, the number and variety of items of office equipment grows also. The equipment of a large modern office of a sizeable church may include sophisticated multiregister bookkeeping machines, perhaps with tape-punch devices for electronic data processing; adding machines and calculators; several electric typewriters—perhaps even an automatic typewriter; copying machines; and dictating machines. The office equipment may also include a high-speed duplicator for stencil, spirit, or offset reproduction (sometimes all three); an electric collator; electric staplers; folding machines; addressing equipment with automatic feed; inserters; and an electric postage meter.

For maintenance work, we are likely to find electric buffers and scrubbing machines, industrial-type vacuum cleaners, well-equipped machine and wood-working shops, and perhaps electric wall-washing equipment. Other equipment may include power mowers, and a fertilizer spreader. As the grounds increase, tractors, electric trimmers, electric hedge clippers, snow blowers, and even electric sweepers are likely to be seen.

The education program may have a roomful of projectors for slides and motion pictures, opaque projectors, electric pencil sharpeners, record players, and public address systems.

Ownership of this equipment requires a considerable investment of church resources, and it is an investment that will have to last a long time.

Because of the large amounts of money involved in procurement of equipment, price is a major consideration. Obviously, however, price cannot be the most important consideration. When we buy equipment, we want the very best machine for the job to be done, regardless of price.

FACTORS AFFECTING EQUIPMENT PURCHASES

In procuring major equipment, therefore, we want to answer five important questions:

1. Considering all church needs, will investment of money in this equipment make the best possible use of our financial resources?
2. Will technical advances soon make superior equipment available?
3. Is the equipment flexible; does it have alternate uses so that we can obtain more value from our investment?
4. Will the volume of work that prompts us to consider buying the equipment continue at a level that will justify the investment of funds for this purpose?
5. Should selection of the equipment be based on the personal preferences of the person who will use it, or should we standardize our equipment to reduce variety?

The uses to be made of equipment should be carefully analyzed and reviewed. Consider duplicating machines. The dictionary refines a duplicator as "a machine for making copies of typed, drawn, or printed matter." This definition embraces the photo-copying machine as well as a spirit duplicator, stencil duplicator, office-size offset duplicator as well as the large offset and letterpress machines of the large commercial printer. Before making a choice, it is important to know what each of these machines requires in terms of preparation and what kind of results we may expect from each.

The photographic copier will make more or less exact duplicates of the original material, but generally very slowly and at a relatively high cost per copy. It cannot be used economically for quantity reproduction. Offset, stencil and spirit duplicating media require prior typing or drawing of a "master" or "stencil," but after such preparation we can make inexpensive copies at high speed and at minimum cost.

To make a choice of duplicating process requires a knowledge and evaluation of the audience as well as of the operator and the program requirements. Two copies of a one-page financial statement may be most satisfactorily made on a photo-copying machine, but, unless the church office is fortunate enough to have an expensive electrostatic copier, 35 copies of this report for the board of directors would most likely be done more economically and efficiently on a spirit duplicator. On the other hand, if copies of this report are to go into permanent archives (spirit duplicating copies do not have long life), a stencil duplicator would be more suitable. Because of its sharper and more dignified appearance, stencil duplicating might also be more suitable for a letter from the minister to all members of the congregation. Finally, for a brochure that will kick off a major fund-raising campaign, nothing short of commercial printing will provide the appropriate professional, prestigeful appearance that is called for.

Knowing the specific needs and program requirements of the church will help the church purchasing agent to choose the kind of reproduction equipment that will best serve the church's needs.

LEASING AND RENTING EQUIPMENT

Tax considerations frequently make the practice of leasing or renting major equipment advantageous to business firms. Since tax considerations do not similarly affect the church, the practice of leasing is less common but can be very useful. For example, when the church is experimenting with a new procedure, it may not wish to purchase expensive equipment until it is sure of its plans. Addressing machines, automatic typewriters, electrostatic copiers, bookkeeping machines, or other needed equipment can often be acquired on a lease-purchase arrangement. Under such an arrangement, part of the rental fee can usually be applied toward purchase of the equipment. The arrangement is similar to a time purchase in that it permits the church to acquire needed equipment without committing large sums.

One advantage of renting or leasing equipment is that the risk of obsolescence is minimized. Since no large capital investment has been made, we have the opportunity of changing to newer and better equipment, even within the lease period. One of the great problems with expensive equipment is the difficulty of justifying the capital loss involved in disposing of it when it has become obsolete. There is a great temptation to keep on using outdated equipment long after it has become inefficient and un-economical. Leasing equipment minimizes this danger.

Another advantage of renting equipment is that, whereas one usually has to contract for service and maintenance of purchased equipment, the renter usually obtains free service and maintenance.

USED EQUIPMENT

The church is often deprived of an opportunity of obtaining needed labor-saving equipment because of the unwarranted stigma that attaches to the word "used equipment." This is unfortunate, because equipment that is obsolete for one specialized purpose may be well suited for another purpose, provided it is in satisfactory condition.

Anyone who has ever purchased a new automobile knows that the market value of major equipment always suffers an immediate sharp drop as soon as there has been an official transfer of title. Thus, a "used" machine of fairly recent vintage can often be bought at a very attractive price.

One advantage of used equipment lies in the fact that the price is free of Federal excise taxes that apply to many items of new equipment.

The safest, although most expensive, way of purchasing used equipment is from a manufacturer who has taken the used machine in trade. Generally, manufacturers will sell the machine only on a "reconditioned" basis. However, such reconditioning usually carries with it a warranty that is only slightly less advantageous than that furnished with the original equipment.

A more attractive price on used equipment can often be obtained in a purchase from a private seller. However, the buyer must include in the price the cost of any repairs necessary to place the equipment in first-class working condition. When purchasing from a private seller, there is generally no warranty. Most likely, cash will have to be paid for the equipment at the time of purchase; therefore, it is important to inspect the equipment before the deal is closed.

DONATED EQUIPMENT

It is not surprising that the churches frequently are the recipient of gifts of equipment and supplies. The spirit that motivates such gifts is a welcome testimony to the loyalty and devotion of members and friends. It is a nostalgic reminder of the traditions of colonial America, where the members of the congregation trooped loyally and devotedly to the simple, unadorned, rural church on the Sabbath, bearing their gifts "in kind" for the support of the church and the sustenance of the minister. In twentieth-century America, however, the donation of merchandise and services to the church sometimes proves to be a mixed blessing.

In a typical case, a businessman whose office is converting from electric bookkeeping to electronic data processing may contribute the older equipment to the church instead of trading it in, selling it on the open market, or disposing of it as scrap. The Government encourages such giving by permitting the businessman to claim a tax benefit for this donation, which may in some cases be equal to or greater than the actual net return that he would realize if he traded or sold the older equipment.

Such gifts should be examined objectively and with great care. The gift of a bookkeeping machine, which might otherwise be beyond its means, may possibly be of great benefit to the church. On the other hand, if the machine is completely unsuited to the church's requirements for effective bookkeeping and fiscal control, it should not accept this gift just because it has been made available by a member.

A difficult question is presented here. On the one hand, rejection of the gift risks antagonizing a member and inhibiting his future generosity. On the other hand, acceptance of a piece of equipment or machinery that is inadequate could in the long run prove to be far more costly to the church, and infinitely more of a handicap than a blessing.

Some congregations have adopted a policy with regard to donated goods that has proved quite successful. All gifts of equipment and merchandise are accepted appreciatively and cordially from any donor, unless the cost of transporting, reconditioning, and installing an item of doubtful utility exceeds its possible salvage value. In the latter case, the donor is thanked but the gift is declined respectfully but firmly. In all other cases, the gift is accepted from the donor with the understanding that the congregation will use it, if feasible, but otherwise will be *free to sell or trade it* for a more suitable item. This usually works out well for both the donor and the church. Through this system, some churches have acquired at nominal, out-of-pocket cost an enviable roster of desirable and useful equipment, some of which it would not otherwise have been able to afford.

SERVICE CONTRACTS

An active debate has been raging for many years over the question of service contracts in the field of administrative management, and it shows no signs of abating. Machines have become increasingly important in the administration of churches. The more important machines become, the more dependent we are on acquiring adequate servicing for them.

As the cost of human labor in all categories has risen, machines have undoubtedly more than paid for themselves. At the same time, the cost of the machines themselves has increased, as has the cost of servicing them.

Few handymen can become skilled in all the intricate service requirements of modern machines and equipment used by most churches. A good maintenance man on the church staff can frequently save expensive service calls by "unjamming" some misaligned address plates, or he may supplement preventive-maintenance calls by blowing dust and lint from the interior of office machines, and he may do wonders in prolonging the life of a lawn mower or landscape tractor. Although preventive care and maintenance of this nature is important, on-going repair and service requires specially trained mechanics.

In arranging for service, we have to make some choices. Should we have the service performed by the manufacturer, or by a local contractor? Regardless of whose facilities we use, do we wish to provide for service on a per-call basis, "as needed," or on a contract basis?

With regard to the first decision (whether to have the service performed by the manufacturer or by an independent service man): a good deal will depend on local conditions and the availability of competent, independent service personnel. Favoring use of the independent service man is the probability that contracts and individual calls may be somewhat less expensive than from the manufacturer's shop. Favoring use of the manufacturer is the probability that the service personnel are better trained in the specifics of the machine involved and are familiar with its changes and improvements. In many cases, this experience and familiarity will more than compensate for any additional cost in service fees. Supporters of this point of view allege that manufacturers of office machinery generally run their service departments at the break-even point or below. Intense competition for sales has forced manufacturers to be alert to the need for adequate service, because if a user feels that he has not obtained adequate or fair service on a machine, he is less likely to buy the same brand when replacing or adding to his equipment.

The decision of whether to keep office equipment under a service contract or to pay for it on a per-call basis will also depend somewhat on the local availability of service personnel and the requirements of the individual office. An important consideration is the amount of money that may be saved in "hidden" costs. Here the crucial factor is "preventive maintenance." Failure to regularly clean and oil an intricate machine can substantially increase the frequency and severity of breakdowns, particularly in the later years of the machine's life. In addition to prolonging the life of a machine, preventive maintenance can materially reduce the amount of time during which the machine is out of service.

To get by without service contracts, the church business office must be sufficiently well organized to maintain a regular and efficient "tickler" file to insure that preventive maintenance service calls will be placed and followed up on a regular time-table basis. This must not depend on one individual's remembering it, and there must be no exceptions because "the machine appears to be in such fine shape right now that it seems a shame to waste the cost of a service call when nothing is wrong." Failing an ironclad assurance of such regularity, the wisest and least expensive course for most churches is to place their equipment under a service contract when the warranty period has expired.

In this connection, it is important to distinguish between *partial* and *complete* coverage by service contracts. Contracts that provide for two or three preventive-maintenance calls a year for oiling and cleaning are less attractive than those that provide for so-called "full coverage." The degree of service furnished without extra cost may vary all the way from the semiannual cleaning and oiling visit, with all repair work and parts chargeable at extra cost, to the so-called full coverage, which, in addition to periodic cleaning, lubrication, and inspection, provides for replacement, at no cost, of worn-out or defective machine parts, platens, and ribbons. It is therefore important to examine the service contract to determine exactly what the annual contract price covers. Costs are relative, and a $25 annual fee for a semiannual inspection and oiling of an electric adding machine, with no free replacement of defective parts, may be relatively more expensive than a $40 annual contract price for full service, with unlimited numbers of service calls and replacement of any worn-out and defective parts. The more complex the machinery, the higher will be both the annual contract price and the per-call rate.

REPAIR PARTS

A service contract with a manufacturer's repair department generally assures the buyer that only genuine repair parts by that manufacturer will be used. The cost of such repair parts are relatively unimportant to the buyer in this case. However, when equipment repairs are made by staff personnel of the church, a decision must be made in each case as to whether to use a "genuine repair part," or what is known in the trade as a "commercial replacement part." In general, it would seem advisable to specify "genuine repair parts" for all parts that have specialized uses, whenever there is the slightest doubt as to which is most appropriate. Thus, in overhauling a four-cycle gasoline engine for a lawn mower, it might be poor economy to substitute a universal type piston ring for one available from the manufacturer of the original motor. On the other hand, one church maintenance man of our acquaintance, who was servicing a large number of small power mowers, found that axles he was acquiring a half-dozen at a time at a cost of $1.95 each as a "manufacturer's part number" were identical to a certain type of ¾″ bolt that was available for 34 cents each from a local hardware supply house.

The same criteria apply to consumable materials used on or by a machine. The manufacturer's brand of duplicating paper, ink, stencils, ribbons, or copying paper may be the best buy. However, with the wide range of competing products, there is no guarantee of such superiority.

DISPOSAL OF OBSOLESCENT AND SURPLUS EQUIPMENT

When a church buys an original item of equipment, the best buy can be determined by a careful evaluation of the price and quality factors discussed in earlier chapters. When replacing a piece of equipment with a newer or more versatile machine, however, an additional factor enters into the determination of value: the amount of money we can recover from the disposal of our old equipment.

Here we have three choices: we can sell the old equipment for scrap; we can trade it in for the new equipment; or we can sell it ourselves on the open market. The first choice is seldom desirable. For almost every item of equipment the church buys, it will generally be offered a trade-in value for its old equipment. However nominal this trade-in price may be, it is almost always more attractive than the amount obtainable for scrap.

The decision of whether to trade in an older model for a new piece of equipment or to sell it privately will vary from item to item and from time to time. A piece of general-purpose equipment, which is usable in a wide variety of locations and uses, may bring a better price on the open market than as a trade-in. Equipment salesmen often advise this procedure. On the other hand, when specialized equipment or very expensive equipment is involved, the direct sale price will be quite attractive only if a user is easily obtainable. If it is sold through a second-hand dealer, it will most likely bring a lower price because of the difficulty of finding a specialized purchaser. In such cases, a trade-in offer is quite likely to be more acceptable, since the dealer for new equipment is trying very hard to make a sale of a high-profit item and will use an attractive trade-in offer as an inducement.

The only way to be absolutely sure that one is getting the best price is to try all three markets: find out the trade-in value; call in a second-hand dealer; and advertise for sale in the newspaper.

One word of caution: as we have already noted, when one purchases used equipment from a private user as opposed to a dealer, one is making a purchase in somewhat of a blind fashion. The merchandise is usually sold on an "as is" basis and no warranty or guarantee can be expected. The same conditions apply to the seller. It is very dangerous for a church selling a used piece of equipment to assume any responsibility for the condition of the merchandise after it has left its possession. Naturally, the church will be honest and furnish to the user all pertinent information about the condition and characteristics of the equipment in question, but the sale itself should be consummated on an "as is, where is" basis.

Chapter 11

SPECIAL PURCHASE PROBLEMS: SERVICES, INSURANCE, JOINT PURCHASE PLANS

OUTSIDE CLERICAL SERVICES

MANY CHURCHES make the mistake of underrating the value of the labor performed by their paid staffs. In trying to apply the "do-it-yourself" technique to church administration they remain the prisoners of the tradition of the little church whose sexton moved the chairs, swept the floor, and kept the records in the sweat-stained lining of his cap.

A generation ago, problems arising from the growing complexity of church administration were solved by employing an office clerk to "take care of all the detail." However modern our church establishments may be today, many of them still are prisoners of the idea that all the "detail" has to be handled by the church's own staff.

Until recently, there was not much choice but the past few years have witnessed a tremendous growth in the number and kinds of specialized services available to the church. One of the best known is the short-term contracting of specialized labor. The yellow pages of even a small-city telephone directory will generally list several agencies that will furnish labor for various skilled tasks, with emphasis on those in the clerical area. Many of these firms will furnish stenographic or typing assistance on a per-hour or per-day basis without the necessity of entering these temporary personnel on your payroll records.

For several years, churches have been able to contract their entire bookkeeping operation to outside firms. A more recent innovation is that of electronic data processing service bureaus. These service bureaus place a small tape or key punch machine in the church office at nominal cost. All transactions are recorded thereon by clerical assistants without special training and are sent to the service bureau for periodic analysis. By farming out these important bookkeeping operations, the church loses some of the advantages of personal control, but it acquires the advantage of an accurate and modern accounting analysis of fiscal transactions at a cost that frequently is lower than that of a well-trained full-time bookkeeper.

Letter shops are prepared to perform for the church every duplicating, binding, addressing, and mailing service required. Also available on a contract basis is the automatic letter writing service. This has become a virtual "must" for fund solicitations, where personalized letters yield far better results than duplicated letters.

Contract clerical services, being very flexible, provide a means of expanding and supplementing the quantity and quality of the church's own operation to any degree desired and almost at will. For any church they provide a source of additional manpower and equipment for short periods or for special jobs. For some churches, clerical contract services can be a complete substitute for the church office in a specific area of work, such as addressing and mailing, taking over the entire job of list maintenance and service.

BUILDING-MAINTENANCE SERVICES

Contract services are also available for maintenance. Window washing is one of the most common. Some churches contract out the general cleaning of halls, sanctuary, and classrooms to firms specializing in this, thereby enabling themselves to retain a minimum maintenance staff. Snow removal from sidewalks and parking lots is often done on a contract basis, as is pest extermination and control, and the laundering of table linen and custodial staff uniforms.

Another important area of contract service covers the maintenance and operation of air conditioning and heating plants. A typical service agreement for the air conditioning and heating plant provides that the service contractor will:

1. Regularly inspect the equipment to check its operation, and oil, clean, and adjust it.
2. Furnish emergency service between regular inspections.
3. Make any repairs, replacements, and adjustments required for satisfactory operation.
4. Furnish and install all necessary repair parts, refrigerant and supplies, including freight and cartage.
5. Provide one summer and one winter change-over per year.

Landscaping services, including fertilizing, tree pruning, and feeding, and lawn maintenance, are also contracted by many churches.

SPECIAL CONSIDERATIONS
IN BUYING INSURANCE

Another volume in this series is devoted entirely to problems involved in assuring adequate insurance coverage for the church. However, since the criteria for establishing value and quality of insurance differ considerably from those for other categories of purchases, we are including here a brief description of some special considerations applicable to church insurance.

To develop a sound insurance program, it is necessary, first of all, to identify all the assets of the church. Included in the assets of a church are its physical facilities, such as buildings and grounds, furnishings, equipment, supplies, money, securities, and automobiles; also its intangibles such as bookkeeping records and other important archival materials that would be expensive or impossible to replace. The record program suggested in Chapter 9 would be helpful in identifying a church's assets for insurance purposes.

Also important is an understanding of some of the perils that would threaten the church with financial loss: fire, lightning, wind, hail, explosion, riot, civil commotion, aircraft damage, vehicle damage, water damage, vandalism and malicious mischief, collapse, flood, glass breakage, theft and embezzlement.

However, one underwriter has stated frankly that no church can afford to buy insurance to protect loss of asset values for "all" exposures or perils of loss. Hence, it is necessary to identify the exposures to be insured. One method is that of classifying the exposures into the following three groups which reflect the degree of financial loss they can inflict on the church:

1. "Must" be insured. This would include the exposures which can cause financial ruin of the church.
2. "Should" be insured. This would include the exposures which, although they may not cause financial ruin, may take up to several years or more to recover fully.
3. "May" be insured. This would include the exposures

which could be an annoyance, but can be handled out of the cash surplus account.

Within this breakdown, each church must make the decision as to the size of dollar loss which meets the test for it. For example, based on its financial status and capabilities, a church may judge that a loss of $10,000 or more would wreck havoc on its operations and that a loss of $100 could be handled easily out of current funds with only a minor annoyance—even if it happened more than once a year. Thus, in deciding which exposures are to be insured, this church should expend its available insurance dollars for coverage of, first, the catastrophic exposures ($10,000 and over); second, the exposures which would place a financial burden on the church ($100–$10,000); and third, the exposures which result in annoyance ($100 and less). In this manner, the most serious exposures are insured first and the church is assured from such an approach that its insurance dollars are being spent wisely and economically.[1]

One recent development in the insurance field is that of combining some of the conventional forms of insurance into a single "package policy." Because of reduced processing costs realized by consolidating as many as six or eight separate policies into a single unit, underwriters can sell "package" policies at a substantial discount. One of the advantages of these packaged policies is that they are so flexible that they can be tailored to meet almost any situation. They may be written in such a way as to keep them in effect until cancelled, without need for further action on the church's part. Numerous methods of premium payment are available.

Although the purpose here is not to recommend specific kinds of insurance for churches we do emphatically sug-

[1] Charles K. Cox, "Church Package Insurance," *Church Management,* February, 1964.

gest the desirability of careful comparison shopping when buying church insurance. Even the smallest church should obtain sample policies from two or more companies. These should be analyzed by an impartial person who is skilled in placing commercial insurance. For the larger church, the services of an independent insurance consultant should be retained. Any church that pays a total annual premium of over $1,500 can expect that a regular review of its insurance program every three to five years will more than pay for itself by assuring the church that it is receiving the advantage of every available benefit.

GROUP-PURCHASING OPPORTUNITIES

Churches can increase their buying power by consolidating their purchase orders with those of similar institutions. By such consolidation churches can take advantage of the price concessions available to users of large quantities. They can also avail themselves of the experience and know-how of professional purchasing agents that larger groups often retain. Although group purchasing often eliminates a certain degree of flexibility in purchases for the church, the advantages of consolidated buying probably outweigh the loss of flexibility.

Protestant group-purchasing opportunities for churches are available through suppliers of denominational literature. Jewish groups are able to take advantage of group procurement of specialized items such as textbooks and some ceremonial objects through the Union of American Hebrew Congregations or the United Synagogue of America. The National Jewish Welfare Board, which provides a group-purchasing plan for Jewish community centers, will sometimes honor requests from individual synagogues for certain types of furniture and equipment.

Some churches take advantage of the large-purchasing

potential of colleges and seminaries related to their denomination. However, such purchases are unusual. The opportunities are limited by the physical distance between the churches and the colleges, and by the complexity of the record keeping that is necessary for such a divided operation.

Few of these group-purchasing opportunities provide the advantages that some observers believe are possible for bulk purchase of a large variety of the goods and services needed by churches. A start in this field is being made by a few small local groups. For example, the Southern California District Council of the Assemblies of God reports (1964) excellent progress in developing its "Builder's Extension Service." This group has the following objectives:

1. To assist our churches with problems associated with building and to help them expedite their building programs.
2. To provide sources for any other commodities.

Probably within the next few years several interested groups—especially the National Association of Church Business Administrators; the Methodist Association of Business Administration; the National Association of Temple Administrators; and the National Association of Synagogue Administrators—will be doing great pioneering work in group purchasing. There seems to be no reason why some of the local chapters of these national groups could not promote the establishment of joint purchasing programs for certain standard commodities and services.

Chapter 12

ETHICS AND PUBLIC
RELATIONS IN
CHURCH PURCHASING

WHY BE CONCERNED WITH ETHICS

THE CHURCH staunchly defends its right and obligation to evaluate business practice in the community. Should not the church, when it enters the market place, be the finest exemplar of good business ethics? Should not each action of the church be above reproach and a living witness of God's word? The end does *not* justify the means, especially if the means are unseemly, dishonest, or in any way unethical.

In the purchasing area, we are concerned with both the personal ethics of individuals engaged in the purchasing process and the institutional standards and policies that guide buyers in their relationships with vendors.

PERSONAL ETHICS OF THE CHURCH
PURCHASING AGENT

There are at least three basic categories of behavior in which questions of personal ethics occur: outright theft and bribery; acceptance of personal favors; and personal purchases.

Outright dishonesty: It would be Pollyannish to pretend

158

that the church is exempt from the kinds of direct theft, embezzlement, and other manifestations of bald dishonesty that each year mulct business establishments of an estimated $2,000,000,000. Although churches generally attract a more highly motivated and basically honest type of person than the average in the general community, all employees of the church are human beings. They are subject to the same temptations and frailties of the flesh that afflict other human beings in our society.

People involved in purchasing for the church, as in purchasing for other organizations, have an opportunity of perpetrating fraud in numerous ways: by conspiring with suppliers who render fictitious invoices for parts, materials, or services that are never delivered; by creating fictitious suppliers who are paid on the basis of false or altered invoices and purchase orders; by direct theft or misappropriation of supplies and equipment for personal use.

Responsible stewardship of congregational property and funds demands that, in our management of congregational affairs, we are neither blinded by unwarranted faith in any individual's incorruptibility nor unwittingly a party to the corruption of any individuals through the mistake of making it too easy for them to succumb to temptation. Periodic, impersonal, outside audits and spot-checks of all aspects of the purchasing and inventory procedure are essential for sound church management.

Acceptance of personal favors: It is very difficult to put down rigid, ironclad rules about ethical standards. These standards will vary from community to community, from business to business, from one part of the country to another. Nevertheless, in the Judaeo-Christian heritage, there are certain fundamental principles of conduct that have become an integral part of our tradition over the ages and that make up the basic ethical standards of our society. There will be disagreement over details and particular applications. The important thing is that the purchasing agent be consistently honest; that he approach each situation with the will and the purpose to act with honesty, integrity, and dignity. He must be ever watchful to insure that his reputation for honesty and integrity is never open to question.

As one basic purchasing source book puts it: "A buyer must rely on a sense of what is right rather than whether something is legal or illegal. Actions must not only *be* right, but must *look* right to other people. A buyer should be conscious at all times of the necessity of keeping himself above suspicion." [1]

It is in this light that the church purchasing agent should evaluate luncheon or dinner invitations, gifts at Christmas or other occasions, or special treatment of any kind from suppliers or prospective suppliers. Outright bribery is not in question here. The individual who succumbs to such wrongdoing will not be bothered by the fine distinctions between where friendship ends and undue influence begins. But the conscientious church purchasing agent will be troubled by such distinctions. The lines are fuzzy enough in normal business situations. In the case of a church, which is organized to be on the receiving end of gifts and contributions, the distinction is both more difficult and more imperative. In determining whether a gift or a favor is proper, it is important to distinguish between what is a gift or a favor to the church and what is a gift or favor to the individual who is functioning on behalf of the church.

In the normal course of business transactions, where time is at a premium, it is frequently desirable to discuss

[1] George W. Aljian, ed., *Purchasing Handbook* (New York: McGraw-Hill Book Co., Inc., 1958), p. 6-4 (sic).

business affairs at the luncheon table. It is unlikely that any church purchasing agent will be corrupted if a salesman picks up a $1.25 luncheon check. But does the same innocence apply to an invitation for the buyer and his wife to share an afternoon of golf and a steak dinner at a fashionable country club? How many years of acquaintanceship entitles a salesman to be considered an old and trusted personal friend?

Similar considerations pertain to the acceptance of tangible gifts. Everyone accepts without question, as a common form of advertising, an inexpensive ball-point pen with the vendor's name imprinted on it. Is a gold-plated pen with the buyer's initials engraved on it an equally innocuous advertising gimmick?

To a certain extent, the question of propriety must be left to the individual, who must retain a certain degree of flexibility in his day-to-day relationships with the people with whom he does business on behalf of the church. But for his protection and guidance a consistent and controlling church rule that applies uniformly to all church representatives and to all church suppliers should be established. In the case of entertainment, the rule might be that the church purchasing agent may accept luncheon hospitality to the limit of $2 per occasion (or some other reasonable figure), but that he may not accept invitations outside working hours. Or, we might forbid the church purchasing agent to permit a supplier to pay his share of any meal. The third alternative might be to authorize and instruct the church representative to offer reciprocal hospitality at luncheon on another occasion as soon as practicable.

The important consideration is that there be a uniform policy applying to such situations, and that the policy be made known to all concerned. Moreover, all persons in-

volved must be scrupulously careful in seeing that the
policy is adhered to both in spirit and in letter.

Purchases for personal use: Purchasing agents are frequently asked to use the buying facilities of the church
to make purchases of a personal nature. There are many
practical objections to such practices. Since the processing
of any purchase order involves expense, such personal purchases represent an indirect but ascertainable cost to the
church. Also it absorbs the time and energy of church
employees. Employee and vendor relations may be affected adversely in the event of complaints or failures of
service of the article bought through this procedure.

In a random sampling of 16 large churches in various
parts of the country, 12 state that they permit no one to
make personal-use purchases through the church account
in order to take advantage of church discounts. Of the four
that do permit such personal-use purchases, two grant the
privilege to only the pastor. The other two permit any
church staff member to receive this advantage.

It would seem that the major ethical consideration in
this practice is the extent to which personal purchases are
sanctioned by the suppliers themselves. Some suppliers
may encourage such business; others may tolerate it reluctantly. If a vendor permits such purchases only because
he is afraid of losing church business, we may well raise
an ethical objection to such transactions.

INSTITUTIONAL ETHICS

Just as the individual who serves as purchasing agent for
his church must avoid not only the fact but also the appearance of unethical practice, so the church itself must
adopt a posture that will be, like Caesar's wife, "above
reproach." It is patently impossible to create rules governing every aspect and nuance of the relationship between

buyer and seller that involves a question of ethics. It is important, however, that all participants in the purchasing process be constantly aware of ethical considerations, to the end that unethical practices are not permitted either by intent or by indirection.

The church has an obligation to any supplier to deal with his sales representatives honestly and frankly. Thus it is unethical to permit a supplier to think he is being considered when the intent is only to "pick his brains," and there is no possibility that he will receive an order. It is also unethical to indicate to a salesman that an initial order at a drastically reduced price will be followed by large-quantity orders when the buyer knows very well that no such future volume is probable. A buyer should not accept a sample of a product from a salesman if he has no intention of giving the product consideration when making future purchases.

Of course, any *deliberate misrepresentation* in negotiating a purchase is strictly taboo. It is equally unethical to engage in the "sharp practice" of permitting a vendor to obtain a false impression of the size of future orders or of any other condition that would induce him to offer a more attractive price, service, or delivery terms. Here again, the cardinal rule is to preserve the appearance as well as the fact of ethical practice.

One of the most common forms of unethical practice is that of taking cash discounts even though the invoices are paid after the discount period has expired. There often is room for disagreement as to whether a 2 per cent cash discount for payment in 10 days should be computed as of the date of the invoice or as of the date of receipt of the goods. However, this is an administrative determination that can easily be worked out with the vendor. In any case, it is clearly improper to take advantage of a cash discount

privilege after the discount period—however computed—
has expired, unless there is explicit concurrence in this
practice by the vendor or his representatives.

The question of *proprietary interest* poses a knotty ethical problem. Does a supplier have a claim on the church's
purchases because he has assisted it in developing a new
idea or a set of practices? A certain church moved to a
large modern plant from an antiquated, run-down building
where all the maintenance work was done by a septua-
genarian janitor. The change presented the newly-em-
ployed business manager with a host of problems in determining the proper equipment and supplies for maintaining
a complex building. The old building was floored completely with worn hardwood planks, but the new building
had a wide variety of terrazzo, parquet, vinyl, rubber, and
asphalt tile. The old painted walls had been supplanted by
marble, ceramic tile, and vinyl wall coverings. In the
myriad of new maintenance problems, one janitor supply
company devoted many valuable hours to demonstrating
the available equipment and the alternative supplies for
maintaining various floor and wall coverings. Eighteen
months later, some disagreement and bad feelings developed between the business manager and the company.
The former, with his newly acquired skill and knowledge,
felt obligated to comb the market for the best possible
value in all janitor supplies. The janitor supply company,
which had developed the initial system, felt that it was
being treated unfairly when it was not retained as the
exclusive supplier. When accepting a new idea, a new
method, or a demonstration of a new practice, the dimension of the proprietary interest that the creative vendor
will have, should be clearly spelled out and thoroughly
understood by both buyer and seller.

Fair treatment of bidders: A cardinal rule of ethical

business practice is that no bid be solicited from a supplier from whom the buyer does not intend to purchase. Preparation of bids or quotations are expensive and time-consuming. It is both dishonest and unfair to use the product of someone else's labor merely for the purpose of affording leverage and pressure on a favored group of suppliers. The confidentiality of a closed bid must be protected, and under no circumstances should any bidder receive privileged information with regard to price or other factors that will assist him in getting the business. Similarly, it is unfair and unethical to permit some bidders to get a second chance after all the proposals have been evaluated.

Reciprocity: One of the most difficult problems facing any church buyer is that of "home preference" for members of the congregation who are suppliers. There are several reasons for arguing that congregation members should receive preferential purchasing attention:

1. Preferential treatment of members often creates good will for the church.
2. Members are likely to give better service to their own church than a disinterested supplier might give.
3. By favoring congregation members, we might encourage them to make donations and gifts that far outweigh any higher prices that may be paid.

The key disadvantage of the home preference rule is that, by limiting purchasing to congregation members, the church frequently excludes more varied offerings. Also, by eliminating competition, the church loses its independence and exposes itself to the possibility of paying higher prices and getting less efficient service.

One congregation, which includes the proprietors of three large janitor supply firms, generally limits its pur-

chases of janitor supplies to these three, submitting a requirements list to them once a year, and placing with the
low bidder a requirements contract for principal categories. In other areas, the rule in this organization is that,
unless there are at least three suppliers on the congregation's membership rolls in any category in which more
than $250 per year is spent, the business manager is in-
structed to seek bids on the open market from a minimum
of three suppliers, including those in his own congregation's membership. It would be just as unethical to exclude
the congregation members from consideration as it would
be to give them exclusivity.

Of the 16 large churches mentioned earlier in this chapter, only one stated that it has a firm policy of favoring
congregation members in placing supply orders. In contrast, one church has an affirmative rule prohibiting purchases of any item from a member of the congregation.
This extreme practice is, at the very least, unusual. It appears to be somewhat punitive to deny a devoted church
member access to his own church's purchase orders on a
basis at least equal to that of other suppliers. It seems
fairly clear that, while very few churches require that
preference be given to suppliers who are members of the
congregation, most church purchasing agents tend to favor
their own members, "all other things being equal." The
ethical imperative here is to be sure that all other things
are *equal*. When a church adopts a clear-cut and well-
publicized practice of insisting on open bidding, and when
this practice is applied with fairness and diplomatic firm-
ness, the best interests of the church are served. Experience has shown that most suppliers understand and cooperate with such a practice when it is promulgated and applied consistently and equitably.

Social justice: The church is the living witness of God's word. When it goes into the market place it must preserve the integrity of its principles of social justice. Thus, it is improper and unethical for a church to attempt to reap temporary advantages by dealing with a vendor who is known to be dishonest and exploitative in his dealing with his employees. It would be equally improper for a church to do business knowingly with business firms whose practices of ethnic or racial discrimination run counter to those goals of social justice the church espouses. Every church has the obligation to be a community leader and exemplar of the highest standards of integrity in both attitude and conduct. The church must never permit itself to be the example of the least common denominator in matters of social and personal ethics.

Increasingly, churches are establishing standards and codes of conduct for members of their congregations. Some have also published codes of institutional conduct. An illustration of one such code is seen in the following statement of administrative policy on racial justice:

1. Our congregation and its auxiliaries will not knowingly patronize or sponsor any activity at a place of public accommodation which discriminates against anyone because of racial, religious, or ethnic origin.
2. Our congregation pursues a policy of nondiscrimination in all relations with our employees.
3. Our congregation will require a nondiscrimination employment clause in any contract to build or improve our physical facilities.
4. Our congregation will not be a party to any restrictive covenant or gentleman's agreement in the purchase, sale, rental, or use of real estate.
5. Our congregation tries to avoid any relationship with

financial institutions and purveyors of equipment, supplies, and services who are known to have discriminatory
policies of any nature.

6. Our congregation will continue to welcome as members
   all persons of our faith regardless of their racial or ethnic
   origins.

It may appear to be a strange commentary indeed that
people engaged in church management need to be re-
minded or instructed in ethical standards and behavior.
The fact is, however, that we who are responsible for
church business affairs are subject to the imperfections
and limitations of other human beings. It is therefore even
more important here than in other areas of human endeavor that we remind ourselves of the high standards of
our Judaeo-Christian heritage. These standards and moral
values must be emphasized and re-emphasized, practiced
and repeated, so that they become instinctive and reflexive.

THE PUBLIC RELATIONS OF ENLIGHTENED
VENDOR RELATIONS

Anything that a church does or says affects, to some degree, its public relations. If its public relations are "good"
its reputation is enhanced, and it is considered a desirable
church with which to be associated and with which to do
business. Consequently, the church's impact for good in
the community is enhanced and supported. If a church's
public relations are "bad," its reputation is diminished and
its influence on the community, and ultimately on its own
members, is reduced. Therefore, each action of the church
purchasing program should result in good public relations.

A church can hardly gain or hold a reputation for integrity and reliability if those selling to it feel that in its
purchasing it is inclined to cheat, or that they cannot de-

pend upon the purchasing department to live up to its promises.

A considerate purchasing agent will avoid wasting both his own time and the salesman's by permitting long interviews that are not related to the business at hand. He will never permit an interview to continue for any length of time after he has determined that there is no possibility that the salesman will be permitted to write an order now or in the future.

Enlightened vendor relations is a key means of influencing the public relations image of the church. In many cases, the purchasing agent is the only representative of the church with whom the vendor will become acquainted. For every salesman to whom he says "yes," he must reject probably a dozen would-be suppliers. For this reason, he should say "no" only in a courteous and friendly manner.

Correspondence and telephone communication can promote good relations in purchasing, as in other business transactions. Their use should not be limited to a denial of an order, a rebuke for improper service, or a request for special service; the church purchasing agent should take every opportunity he has to say "thank you" by telephone or correspondence for service diligently rendered and orders promptly and efficiently handled. Good manners, good taste, and spontaneous friendliness are never misplaced.

TESTIMONIALS AND ENDORSEMENTS

Testimonials and endorsements also have important public relations and ethical implications. Letters of appreciation to vendors for outstanding service and for products of unusually high quality will almost always be used by them in soliciting new business. The salesman will often show such letters to prospective customers, and if the church's recommendation is a factor in additional sales, the church's reputation and public relations image become identified with those of the supplier. Therefore written commendations to suppliers should be judiciously given, and only when they are truly deserved.

In addition to such *informal* uses of written commendations, many vendors will attempt to receive *formal* testimonials and endorsements from a church purchasing agent for their product and service, and will request permission to use such endorsements in printed brochures and other advertising. There is nothing intrinsically wrong in issuing such testimonials or endorsements when they are deserved, but it should be recognized that their use in certain contexts could become embarrassing to the church. In issuing such formal testimonials or endorsements, therefore, the church should always reserve the right to approve the specific uses to be made of such commendations.

The church's endorsement should never be available on a fee basis. The reputation and public image of a church is too precious to be obtainable for a price. For a church to sell a testimonial would smack too much of commercial bribery to be considered an ethical public relations practice.

Chapter 13

A MANUAL OF
PURCHASING POLICY
AND PROCEDURE

Purchasing is an extremely important phase of church business management. As administrative instruments for prudent stewardship of church resources, we must keep in mind the fact that the manner in which we carry out the purchasing activity affects and is affected by the various programs of the church. All members of the church staff, whether employees or volunteers, are involved in some way with the spending of church money and the acquisition of goods and services. We have pointed out how essential it is that each of these persons base his actions on knowledge and purpose, so that the money spent by the church will provide the strongest possible support of its mission. To insure this, there must be common understanding and consistent implementation of policy, rules, and procedures for purchasing.

NEED FOR A MANUAL ON PURCHASING

The purpose of a church purchasing manual is to provide an explicit description of the way the purchase function will be carried out within the church, and, equally important, the way in which purchasing will relate to individuals and groups outside the church. It is an administrative instrument for promulgating policy and procedure.

Admittedly, most churches will find it possible to operate without a formal written manual of this nature. There are, however, a number of advantages that make an official purchase manual desirable. Such an instrument:

1. Facilitates the making of decisions about important questions concerning the purchase of goods and services.
2. Gives some assurance that careful advance thought will be given to difficult problems.
3. Anticipates difficult situations and suggests how problems arising from them can be solved in a calm, reasoned atmosphere, divorced from a sense of urgency.
4. Provides a basis for common understanding of church policy and for consistency in its application.

SOURCES OF CHURCH POLICY

Where do church policies governing purchasing come from? Some come from recorded decisions of the church board. These establish the manner in which the church solves certain problems, and usually they can be considered policy for action on similar problems arising in the future. Additional policies can be derived from the basic law of the church, the charter, or the constitution and by-laws. In some cases, certain policies are determined by the denominational structure. Policies governing purchasing practices often are developed from various separate decisions, which, when taken together, form a body of precedent for similar action in the future.

All of these together, when set forth logically and coherently in a single document, can be described as the church manual on policy and procedure of purchasing. A little time spent in assembling such a manual will pay large dividends in terms of consistency, clarity, and efficiency of the purchasing procedure.

A REALISTIC MANUAL OF POLICY AND PROCEDURE

The following hypothetical manual of policy and procedure might have been prepared for a church of 750 member families, in a small city on the fringe of a large metropolitan area. The form and content are suggestive only, but it can easily be adapted to the specific needs of a particular church.

MANUAL OF PURCHASING POLICY AND PROCEDURE FOR THE UNIVERSAL COMMUNITY CHURCH

(Approved by Board of Trustees, January 15, 1965)

This manual is intended to serve as a guide to church staff and lay volunteers in implementing the policies and procedures under which all purchases are to be made for the Universal Community Church. In carrying out the purchasing responsibility, every effort will be made to acquire needed goods and services in the appropriate quantity, at the proper time, and at the most economical price. The primary aim will be to promote the avowed purposes of our congregation, consistent with strict adherence to the ethical imperatives of our faith.

Responsibility for Purchasing: The business manager is hereby designated the chief purchasing agent. He is responsible for coordinating the procurement of all materials, supplies, equipment, and services needed by all personnel, departments, and affiliates.

Limitations on Purchase Authority: Purchase orders for amounts up to $150 may be made on the signature of the business manager only. Purchases in excess of that amount must be authorized also by the chairman of the using department and the chairman of the finance committee. Petty cash purchases may not exceed $10 for any one purchase without advance written authorization of the business manager.

Requisitions: In general, requests for items to be purchased shall be made on the appropriate requisition form. In emergencies, where it is physically difficult or impractical to execute a written requisition, an oral requisition may be accepted at the discretion of the business manager, and this fact shall be noted on the purchase order.

Purchase Orders: Save for such exceptions as are noted below, no purchase agreement shall be made except on a standard purchase order form. In case of emergency, a purchase order number may be conveyed orally to the supplier, but, wherever practical, confirmation shall be made by a formal purchase order.

Emergency or Petty Cash Purchases: Sales slips for all items purchased out of petty cash on an emergency basis shall be verified by a petty cash slip, approved by the business manager. The original sales slip or receipt shall be attached.

Budgetary Authorization: All requisitions and purchase orders shall carry the appropriate budgetary account number. The requisition shall be initialed by the head of each using department, who will thereby certify that the purchase is within the budgetary allotment authorized for this purpose. If a purchase exceeds the budgetary allotment, the requisition must be approved by the chairman of the finance committee before the purchase order is issued.

Vendor Relations: All salesmen and other representatives of vendors who call on our church will be treated courteously, fairly, and without prejudice. However, in order to conserve the time of church staff personnel, salesmen are requested to limit their calls to the hours of 9:30 A.M. to 11:30 A.M. on Tuesdays and Thursdays, except by special appointment.

Bids and Quotations: Bids and quotations will be solicited only from companies that are likely to be considered in awarding orders or contracts. Information received from bidders will not be used to play one supplier against another nor to offer advantages to favored suppliers.

Home Preference: Everything else being equal, the Universal Community Church will give preference to suppliers who are members of our congregation. *However, member preference will be exercised only after ALL value factors, such as quality, price, service, and delivery schedules have been evaluated and it is determined that these factors are indeed equal to those available from other sources.* The buying goal of our church is to obtain maximum value for each dollar expended.

Cash Discounts: Suppliers will be informed that invoices providing for cash discounts will be processed for payment in the shortest practicable period and will generally be paid before invoices which provide no inducements for speedy payment. However, cash discounts will not be taken unless they have been actually earned. In the absence of a discount for earlier payment all merchandise and services which have been received in good order will be paid for within 30 days following receipt of an invoice.

Acceptance of Gifts: Suppliers are requested not

to tender gifts or gratuities to any employee or representative of the church. Suppliers wishing to make such gifts may contribute them to the church instead. Church representatives are encouraged to reciprocate any luncheon entertainment that may be offered by suppliers and may request reimbursement from the petty cash fund for such expenditures.

Personal Purchases: Personal purchases from our suppliers at preferred prices will be made for members of the church staff only with the full knowledge and consent of the supplier involved. The church will not accept responsibility for quality, price, or service when such purchases are made for staff members.

Ethical Practice: Representatives of the church are expected to assure themselves that all purchasing activities conform in every respect to the highest standards of ethics and moral values of our faith, that they avoid all aspects of "sharp practice," and that they adhere rigidly to all tenets of ethical business practice and social justice as proclaimed by our denominational authorities and by our Board.

POLICY AND PROCEDURE FOLLOW-UP

The suggested policy and procedure manual outlined above is suggestive only and touches on only a few of the many points that could be included in a church purchasing manual. However, no manual is more effective than its follow-up. Procedures are not self-executing and will be ignored unless they are realistically related to the dimensions of the job at hand, and unless they are understood and accepted by the people involved. The requirements must be kept simple enough to be meaningfully executed, and there must be constant follow-up to see that all elements of the procedure are followed.

Chapter 14

BY WAY OF SUMMARY

IN THIS BOOK—the first ever published on the subject of church purchasing—we feel a special obligation to answer these three basic questions: To whom is this book directed, and to whom is it not directed? How will it promote effective church management? What are its limitations or boundaries?

This book is for those who are responsible for administering business affairs of churches. It is not intended for persons engaged in management of commercial enterprises, government agencies, schools or colleges, hospitals, or other organizations. A church is none of these, although in some respects it is similar to all of them.

Our central objective is to present some general principles of management that can be applied effectively in purchasing for the church. Some are the same as, or similar to, those applied generally in business. In a few cases, successful church purchasing demands approaches that are unique and specifically relevant to the nature, purposes, and goals of the church.

This book is based on two major premises: First, if churches are to accomplish their purposes effectively, their purchasing function must be performed as well as, or better than, that of other organizations. Second, since churches are service-rendering rather than profit-making, and because of their voluntary nature and the trustee relationship involved, their purchasing procedures must differ in certain respects from those of commercial enterprises; and the differences must be clearly indentified and thoroughly understood.

We recognize that the purchasing function is closely related to budgeting, fund raising, office management, record keeping, personnel management, and property management. Nevertheless, we have avoided detailed discussion of these other aspects of church administration except where they are immediately and specifically relevant to church purchasing.

The following "key" ideas presented in the foregoing chapters are, we believe, the basic framework within which any effective system of church purchasing should operate:

1. *Effective purchasing is important for all churches.* Every church, *regardless of size,* already has some system of acquiring goods and services. Each church, large or small, has the obligation of gearing its present system of purchasing to an orderly and efficient procedure of acquiring the best value for each dollar expended.

The author's experience in purchasing for congregations of various sizes convinces him of the importance of thoughtfully-designed purchasing procedures, realistically related to the needs of the specific church. We have, therefore, tried to make this volume applicable to both large and small congregations and have endeavored to make necessary distinctions. However, since "large" and "small" are relative concepts, the reader, before discarding any suggestion as impractical for his church, should apply four test questions:

    a. What specific objections exist?

    b. How could the church benefit if the suggestion were practical?

    c. What probably would happen if the suggestion were adopted on a trial basis?

    d. If the suggested procedure seems impractical how can it be adapted to our unique requirements?

2. *Responsibility and control should be precise:* An effective system of church purchasing centralizes the buying activities and pinpoints responsibility for carrying them out. This centralized function and responsibility should be delegated to a qualified purchasing agent, who should be someone other than the pastor. Whether he or she be a layman serving in a volunteer capacity, or a professional business manager, the purchasing agent must be resourceful, diplomatic, thorough, and endowed with an abundance of "common sense." The purchasing agent must be accorded requisite authority for consolidating requirements and purchases and for making final determination of the factors that enter into the "best buy."

3. *Church purchasing should be comprehensive.* Church purchasing begins with an expression of need for goods or services and provides machinery for accomplishing, in an orderly manner and with a minimum of waste motion, each basic element of the purchasing process: determination of quality, quantity, timing, price, and sources of supply; placement and follow up of the order; receipt, storage, and distribution of goods. Effective church purchasing achieves maximum economy and efficiency through centralization and consolidation.

4. *Good purchasing is kept simple.* Being complete and comprehensive does not require a complex system. We need adequate forms to aid in requisitioning, obtaining price quotations, placing purchase orders, and in keeping track of what we have bought and from whom. But we do not make three copies of a requisition form when two serves our purpose;

we studiously avoid making paperwork and record-keeping a goal in and of itself.

5. *The "best buy" is a goal of church purchasing.* The church seeks to acquire maximum value for its expenditure of money and energy; that is, it endeavors to obtain the "best buy." But "value" is not an isolated and independent factor. It is relative to both quality and price: the higher the price and the lower the quality the less the value. Value is also closely related to function. An item is not simply *good,* but is good *for* something. A church school that publishes a two-color monthly newsletter for its 1,000 students might find that a duplicator which prints only 2,500 sheets an hour, but has color drums that can be changed quickly and cleanly, is more functional, and thus a better value, than a similarly-priced duplicator that prints 5,000 sheets an hour, but that has a messy and cumbersome method of changing ink color.

6. *Purchasing is a supportive function.* Church purchasing is not an end in itself, but a means to an end. It undergirds and bolsters the various programs of the church. It encourages responsible stewardship of the church's material resources so as to give maximum power and thrust to the church's programs. In carrying out the purchasing function of a church, every transaction must reinforce the church's spiritual goals. Therefore, the church must consistently demand the highest possible standards of ethical conduct in its corporate activities, from its purchasing agent and from its suppliers.

In the market place, as from the pulpit, every action of the church must communicate a concept of divine mission to inspire and elevate our society. A church whose purchasing practices help achieve this goal is blessed indeed.

QUESTIONS FOR STUDY AND REVIEW OF PURCHASING FOR THE CHURCH

by Hugh G. E. Paull *

THE PURPOSE of the following questions is to serve as an aid to mastery of the content of Julian Feldman's new book on church purchasing. They are based on "A Guide to Systematic Study of Purchasing for the Church," a portion of a syllabus for a course offered by the School of Business Administration, The American University, Washington, D.C., and are used in Mr. Feldman's book by special permission.

Some of the questions have been modified or rearranged to bring them into better relation to Mr. Feldman's book. A few are answered, at least partially, in the Editor's Introduction. Others suggest ideas that, for justifiable reasons, are not treated explicitly in this book. Diligent search for comprehensive answers to these questions should lead to a deeper appreciation of procedures that churches could use effectively in procuring goods and services.

1. What distinctive purposes and functions of individual churches make them significantly different from (a) other non-profit organizations, (b) com-

---

* Director of Business Administration, First Baptist Church, Washington, D.C.: member of the Part-time Faculty of the School of Business Administration, The American University.

mercial establishments, (c) government agencies?

2. Which of the terms—purchasing, procurement, and acquisition—is the most appropriate for use in church business management? Give your reasons.

3. In what respects would the non-profit character of a church influence its policies and practices of acquiring goods and services needed in accomplishing its objectives and goals?

4. Explain how the voluntary nature of a church would influence its policies and practices of acquiring items needed in accomplishing its objectives and goals.

5. What are the duties and responsibilities of the chief governing body of your church? What powers of delegation does it have? Which three of the following words best describe the scope of its task: policy, procedure, process, program, plan? What should be its role in procurement of goods and services?

6. What advantages and disadvantages do you believe would result from centralizing the business management functions of your church? How would each of the following groups be affected: woman's society, Sunday school, youth organizations, men's Bible class, the agency responsible for the "poor of the parish," the employed staff? Answer this question again, substituting the word "acquisition" for "business management."

7. Suggest and describe two plans, either of which, in your opinion, most churches could use satisfactorily in effecting a transition from a decentralized to a centralized form of purchasing.

8. Do you believe that (a) only large churches realize any benefits from centralized purchasing, (b) de-

centralized purchasing is more flexible than centralized systems, (c) effective purchasing depends on good inventory control? Defend your viewpoints.

9. Give some examples of how a central purchasing agent can abuse his authority. What are some of the "pitfalls" to be avoided in a centralized system of church purchasing? How are they avoided?

10. What, in your opinion, are the significant characteristics of an effective program of church purchasing? Give reasons in support of your opinions.

11. Describe by example how each of the following processes is used in a church purchasing operation: forecasting, planning, organizing, controlling, reporting.

12. In your opinion, what are the principal reasons why systematic purchasing for churches has assumed greater importance in recent years?

13. What are the duties and responsibilities of the church purchasing agent?

14. What basic authorities should be vested in the church purchasing agent?

15. Prepare a suggested description of a proposed position of volunteer purchasing agent for an 800-member church with a multiple staff that includes a full-time employee who serves in the dual capacity of director of education and business manager.

16. What kinds of information would a church purchasing agent need, and from what sources might help be available, in buying furniture and equipment for a new education building now under construction?

17. By what criteria would you evaluate the effectiveness of the purchasing program of an individual church?

18. Which of the following factors control the volume of church purchasing: (a) program limitations, (b) market shortages, (c) available financial resources? Explain your answer.

19. How is stewardship reflected in the purchasing practices of churches?

20. Describe the system by which your church (or some other church) assures itself that (a) an item should be purchased, (b) the right thing is selected, and (c) the desired article was properly delivered and should be paid for.

21. Trace a hypothetical transaction through the seventeen steps in the procurement procedure. Identify each step as it is reached.

22. What kinds of materials and services ordinarily are purchased by your church in a twelve-month period? How are new products introduced so as to create a "need"? Who determines quality? Quantity? Price? Who does most of the buying? Why?

23. What do purchasing agents mean by lead time? MRO items? Quality control?

24. What constitutes "purchase authorization"? How much specification should the purchase requisition contain? To what extent should the purchasing agent be bound by the requisitioner's specification of quantity, quality, vendor, urgency, program adaptability, availability of funds? What form must be used in transmitting the requisition in a church with a $20,000 per year budget?

25. Show how a repeating requisition can save time, storage, and money.

26. What is meant by the "small-order problem"? What is the "large-order problem"? What factors must be

considered to establish the size of an order that will be both efficient and economical?

27. Do you agree (a) that purchasing name brand items is usually easier than buying unbranded items, (b) that the more rigid the specifications the more certain the church can be that the goods ordered will be usable, (c) that the head of the using department is most likely to be the best judge of what is needed and from whom it should be purchased? Give reasons for your answers.

28. What are cash discounts? What is their essential purpose? Of what benefit are they to the customer? What are some other types of discount?

29. What factors, other than the quoted price, enter into cost?

30. Distinguish between "vendor" and "source of supply." By what principal methods, suitable to churches, are vendors selected? What preference should be shown to suppliers who are members of the congregation?

31. Describe a suitable filing system for sales catalogs and direct mail brochures in a one-secretary church office.

32. Who should authorize payment of invoices, and what supporting documents should be present?

33. What should constitute minimum receiving and storage facilities in any church?

34. Name and describe any two types of inventory control that may be used advantageously in churches. Indicate by examples two situations in which each type may be suitable.

35. When equipment becomes surplus through replacement, should the purchasing agent be responsible

for disposing of it? If not, to whom should the problem be assigned? Give reasons for your answer.

36. What situations might justify the purchase of used equipment for a well-financed and managed church? Suggest equally valid reasons for buying new equipment. Give examples of three kinds of equipment in each category.

37. What situations might justify leasing equipment? Give examples of five kinds of equipment customarily leased to churches.

38. What advantages and disadvantages can be derived from cooperative purchasing arrangements among churches? Name three common cooperative purchasing organizations.

39. Identify some concepts and procedures of purchasing that have been applied successfully in commercial enterprises, but are not appropriate for churches.

40. What are some of the ethical, moral, and theological implications of church purchasing?

41. From your reading or from actual observation, describe a situation that illustrates lack of consideration of ethics in purchasing for a church. How could the unethical action have been avoided?

42. Select three individual churches, preferably from three different denominations, and from each obtain a description of the church's system for purchasing goods and services. What conclusions do you draw from this experience?

43. How frequently and for what reasons should purchasing procedures be systematically reviewed?

44. Devise a "flow chart" of church purchasing procedures, indicating necessary authorities, controls, ac-

tions, forms, and documents. Is your answer to Question 21 consistent with this chart?

45. What significant developments or trends in church purchasing do you predict or suggest for the decade immediately ahead?

INDEX

Here is a unique guide for those involved in spending church funds.

This volume explains effective organization for church purchasing, the merits of centralizing the purchasing functions, and the selection of sources and choice of a supplier.

The author explains, in easy to understand terms, the various legal aspects of church purchasing as well as the ethics involved. He provides expert details on: forms and methods for making requisitions, getting competitive bids, authorizing the purchase, checking the invoice, inventory controls, maintaining proper records, replacing equipment, and trade-in items.

In addition, there are discussions on such subjects as fraud, understanding of warranties, tax exemption, vendors and suppliers and joint purchasing techniques. Included are specific forms, suggested methods and procedure.